THE
LITTLE GIANT BOOK
Eerie Unspeakable Chills

By Sheila Anne Barry, C. B. Colby,
Ron Edwards & John Macklin

Sterling Publishing Co., Inc.
New York

Library of Congress Cataloging-in-Publication Data Available

10 9 8 7 6 5 4 3 2 1

Published by Sterling Publishing Co., Inc.
387 Park Avenue South, New York, NY 10016
© 2004 by Sterling Publishing Co., Inc.
Material in this book previously appeared in *World's Best
"True" Ghost Stories* © 1988 by Sterling Publishing Co., Inc.;
World's Most Mysterious "True" Ghost Stories © 1996 by
Ron Edwards; *World's Most Mystifying "True" Ghost Stories*
© 1997 by Ron Edwards; *World's Most Spine-Tingling "True"
Ghost Stories* © 1992 by Sheila Anne Barry, and *World's
Strangest "True" Ghost Stories* © 1991 by Sterling Publishing Co., Inc.
Illustrations © by Elise Chanowitz and Jim Sharpe.
Distributed in Canada by Sterling Publishing
c/o Canadian Manda Group, 165 Dufferin Street
Toronto, Ontario, Canada M6K 3H6
Distributed in Great Britain and Europe by Chris Lloyd at Orca Book
Services, Stanley House, Fleets Lane, Poole BH15 3AJ, England
Distributed in Australia by Capricorn Link (Australia) Pty. Ltd.
P.O. Box 704, Windsor, NSW 2756, Australia

Printed in China
All rights reserved

Sterling ISBN 1-4027-1546-3

Contents

Tales of Terror 321

Ghostly Animals 333

Index 349

Ghosts in the House

Why is a house haunted? Why does a ghost need to remain in it, endlessly repeating the same actions? The hauntings in this chapter are of vastly different types, but every one of them reveals the obsession of a troubled spirit. What should be done with a ghost in the house?

The Screaming Room

It was a small house in a poor neighborhood in Sussex, England—nothing fancy and not very old. But what happened there was macabre.

The year was 1947. World War II was over, and it was hard to find a place to live. Helen and her brother, Hank, had just been discharged from the army, and they were delighted to find the little house, even if it was less than half furnished. They were both used to roughing it, and it was really great to have a whole house to themselves. They each invited a friend to visit for a few weeks.

Helen took the best room, the one on the second floor. It was the largest and had a real bed, not just an army cot. She settled down to sleep with an ecstatic

sense of comfort. In the middle of the night she woke up. The room was dark. This was not unusual, she thought, but did it seem darker than normal? And there was a heaviness, a stillness. She had a strong feeling that something was there with her.

"You're being ridiculous," she told herself. "You're just not used to having a room to yourself."

But she couldn't get back to sleep. She began to sweat and to see shapes in the blackness, and a cold terror crept over her. She forced herself to reach out and switch on the light. The room was ugly, but no one was in there with her—no one she could see.

The same thing happened the next night. Helen began to dread going upstairs.

Then the third night, she awakened with a sudden shock and sat straight up in bed. The room was vibrating with sound, as if a scream had just ended and was reverberating through the air. Was the room screaming, or was it her own scream, or did it come from downstairs?

Helen leaped out of bed and rushed down the stairs. As she did, she heard a strange clicking sound. But Hank and their friends were all sound asleep.

The next day, Helen suggested that it would be easier for her to start breakfast in the morning and lock up at night if she slept downstairs.

"What? Give up the best room?" Hank said. "Well, none of that noble self-sacrifice for me. I'm moving upstairs into that room before you change your mind."

Hank lasted three days in the upstairs room. Then he said, not looking Helen in the eye, it was

12

really only right for their guest to have the best room. So he moved out and his friend William moved upstairs.

The next morning when William came down to breakfast, both Hank and Helen looked at him closely. He seemed tired, but he said he had slept well, and he got quite irritated with their questions.

William's temperament did not improve as the days passed. He grew more and more distant, red-eyed and silent, and spent increasing amounts of time in the room. Then, when he had been visiting the house for exactly two weeks, he started screaming, one bloodcurdling scream after another.

Neighbors called the police, but they couldn't quiet him. At last a doctor put him under sedation and he was taken by ambulance to a mental hospital, where he spent the next year.

Jennifer, Helen's friend, was so shaken that Helen had to spend the next couple of weeks taking care of her. A few months later, Jennifer attempted suicide and she, too, was taken to a mental hospital.

Hank and Helen finally talked about the room. Why hadn't they discussed it before? They admitted they thought they'd be laughed at. They had both heard the screaming, and Hank claimed he had felt the presence of some kind of horrible "cat thing."

Helen at last got thoroughly sick herself, so it wasn't until some months later that she talked with one of the neighbors about the house. It had originally been built as a bungalow by a small commercial builder who added the upstairs room later. He divided the house in half, renting out the right half to an old woman and her daughter and living in the left. He soon moved on, but the daughter of the old woman had become obsessed with spiritualism and used to experiment with a Ouija board. What ghastly, inhuman thing had she unleashed?

"Where can I find her?" Helen asked.

"Won't do you any good to find that one," said her neighbor. "They carted her off to the madhouse, they did, just a few weeks before you and your brother moved in."

The Case of the Possessive Poltergeist

Do poltergeists have emotions the way people do? Can they become so jealous of the people they haunt that they don't want them to go out or have any friends? That seems to be what happened in the case of the dish-throwing poltergeist of Nelly Roca.

In took place in the bayou country near New Orleans in 1963. Nelly Roca had just moved into a mobile home. She was about to serve dinner one night to a few friends when plates began to leap out of the cupboard. One by one they hurled themselves or rather, were hurled by something, across the room. Every plate Nelly owned was shattered.

It took a few days before she was willing to go back inside the mobile home. She brought a friend and more plates, and they made some coffee. Then, at exactly eight o'clock, the cups and saucers started

dancing around on the table until, one by one, they crashed down on the floor. Nelly's friend beat a hasty retreat.

A few days later, Nelly was asked to leave the mobile home. Rumors were going around, she was told, and if word were to get out about the ghost, it wouldn't be good publicity for the trailer park.

About a month later, Nelly had settled into a small apartment and was in the living room talking with some friends. They heard sounds from the kitchen. You guessed it—dishes were jumping off the shelves and then, one by one, were being thrown *by something* against the walls and smashing on the floor.

It was becoming clear that the ghost or poltergeist, or whatever it was, was not going to tolerate Nelly having guests. But Nelly had no intention of isolating herself. She bought a set of plastic dishes, and that seemed to solve the problem for a while.

Then, on the April, 5, 1964, Nelly went to a friend's house to visit. The poltergeist evidently went also. No sooner had she walked in when the dishes on the kitchen table began to shake and the plates on the shelves began to smash against the walls. Nelly's friend said, "Nelly, for pity's sake, get out of here!" and Nelly rushed away. As soon as she left, the dishes stopped moving.

Obviously, Nelly was no longer being asked out very much. Finally, in January 1965, she was invited to a small housewarming, and it happened again. Plates, cups and saucers, and bowls all began flying around the kitchen. Nelly didn't have to be asked to leave. She got out, and the destruction stopped.

Every time Nelly Roca went out or had any company, dishes went berserk.

Finally, in August, she and a few of the friends she had left went to consult Harry Citron, a voodoo priest who lived deep in the bayou country. She sat down in a shack with Citron and his disciples, who carried torches and strangely marked boxes. One of the boxes contained plates and bowls, which were put on small tables around Nelly.

As usual, the plates and bowls began to shake and be thrown on the floor. The priest and his disciples started chanting and formed a circle around Nelly. One of the disciples lifted a second box and held it up with the lid open. Plates were thrown at the box but missed. Then one plate rose, as if someone were picking it up and attempting to place it in the box. The priest shook a gourd and lunged toward the box. Quickly, the disciples slammed the lid on and nailed it shut. The poltergeist was trapped in the box.

Nelly Roca never had trouble from it again.

The Octagon Hauntings

Who is the ghost that resides in the famous Octagon House in Washington, D.C.? Is it the shade of a young suicide? Or the wife of a great president?

The eight-sided brick mansion, built in 1798, stands on the corner of New York Avenue and Eighteenth Street. Now the national headquarters of the American Institute of Architects, it was designed by Dr. William Thornton, who also designed the Capitol. Originally, it was built for a Colonel John Tayloe of Mount Airy, Virginia. Later President James Madison and his wife, Dolley, lived there.

The entrance hall of the Octagon is circular, with curved doors and windows to fit the round walls. Running up to the top of the three-story building from the center of the next hall is a spiral staircase

that plays an important part in one story of the Octagon ghost.

The circular entrance foyer extends up through the house, providing a round room on each floor, including the basement. Just outside the basement wall, there is a brick-lined, arched tunnel that comes to a dead end after 20 feet. It is assumed that this tunnel once led to a small creek or bayou along the Potomac River, but no one really knows. . . .

For example, according to another ghost legend—as we shall see—this tunnel may once have led directly to the White House a few blocks away. Through it, Dolley Madison is said to have carried valuables, including the famous unfinished Gilbert Stuart painting of George Washington, to keep them safe when the British set fire to the White House in 1814.

According to the first ghost legend, one of Colonel Tayloe's 15 daughters ran off and was married against his wishes. When she returned to ask his forgiveness, wearing lilacs in her hair, he said he never wanted to see her again. Without a word, she climbed to the top of the great stairwell and plunged, screaming, to the lower hall and death. It is said that to this day, on rare occasions, one can still hear that scream—and the crash of her body to the first floor.

On other days, Octagon visitors smell lilacs, another sign that the suicide ghost is close by.

Competing for status with Miss Tayloe's shade, of course, is that of Dolley Madison—who, when lilacs are sniffed and screams and crashes are heard, is said to be running through the basement tunnel in a panic, in her haste occasionally dropping Washington's portrait with a resounding crash!

The Lady on the Stairs

New Orleans is known for Mardi Gras festivals, delicious Creole cuisine, and Dixieland jazz. It also has the distinction of being the most haunted city in America. There are many opinions about which house is the most haunted, but one structure built in 1830 has an especially intriguing resident.

The two-and-a-half-story house at 2606 Royal Street has French doors, a large fireplace, a winding stairway, and a beautiful Creole lady with long dark hair who glides down the stairs. The lovely woman, wearing a V-neck lace dress, died more than 100 years ago.

Some have seen the brown-eyed phantom in the rooms. One occupant, lying in bed one evening, thought he saw his wife standing at the door. Before he could speak, he felt movement in the bed and turned to

see his wife beside him. Quickly, he looked across the room, but the image was gone.

While climbing the stairs, one man was forced to step aside and allow the dark-haired lady to pass. As she moved by, the terrified man felt an icy chill and rushed to his bedroom, quickly locking himself in.

One evening a woman heard the cries of her infant grandchild. Upon entering its room she was surprised to see a lovely woman in a lace dress bending over the crib. When the grandmother called out, the mysterious woman walked through a wall.

Unpleasant things have befallen some who have seen the strange vision. One young man was killed in an automobile accident right after meeting the lovely ghost on the stairs. Another man became so emotionally disturbed that he tried to commit suicide.

Some residents have heard the midnight moans of a woman crying in the attic, though that area of the house has been sealed off for years.

The apparition is believed to be the spirit of Madame Mineurecanal, a Creole lady who hanged herself over the staircase in the early 1900s.

Haunted Ferreby House

Sometimes greed reaches even beyond the grave. Perhaps this is what happened in the case of the mansion known as Hopsfield. It got its name because it stood in the middle of a field of hops outside the town of Waterlooville in Hampshire, England.

A huge, rambling, Gothic-style house, it was built by a Ferreby in the early 1800s. Proud of his mansion, which boasted a long flight of stone steps to the front door, Mr. Ferreby was determined to have it stay in the family forever: It must never change hands. It would always be home to the Ferrebys. That was his dying wish.

The Ferreby offspring lived in the house and raised their children in it. But when the grandchildren were grown, and their parents had died, they wanted nothing to do with the old place. The rooms had always seemed dank and cold and the atmosphere was heavy and oppressive.

After moving out, the Ferrebys rented the house to a group of Spiritualists, who weren't there long before they began complaining that the ghost of old Mr. Ferreby kept appearing, shaking with anger and threatening them. They were so terrified that they asked for and received permission to sublet the house.

The new occupants were a widow and her daughter, then in her twenties. They stayed only a short while. The mother was found dead in her bed at one o'clock in the morning. Soon afterward, the daughter moved out of the grim old house, which by this time had begun to get a sorry reputation.

No one else wanted to rent the house. But the Ferreby heirs were able to sell it. It was bought almost immediately by a newly retired sea captain and his wife. One of the captain's treasures was a collection of Indian daggers he had gathered on his travels. He now kept them in a display case in the hall of the Ferreby house.

One morning the sea captain was found lying dead in the front hall, one of his Indian daggers buried in his back. His widow moved out immediately, leaving behind a mystery that the police couldn't solve. Only the local people claimed to know what had happened: Old Ferreby's ghost, long in his uneasy grave, was the killer.

By this time no local person would think of going near the old house. But in the 1920s it caught the eye of the Dalton family, who were determined to buy it even against the advice of advisors and friends. The old Gothic-style building appealed to Mr. Dalton. The dark gloominess of its interior, he said, was the result of neglect. The rooms could be renovated and the atmosphere improved. He poured money into the house, transforming it into a beautiful and luxurious home, but he was never able to get rid of the strange chill that seemed to pervade it.

Overnight guests of the Daltons remember uneasy nights—strange noises, doors that were opened by invisible hands, children who woke in the middle of the night to find themselves crammed under their beds. And everyone still complained of the cold, oppressive atmosphere that no amount of renovations would change.

But there was no discussing these things with the Daltons. They had ready explanations. Children do strange things in their sleep; old houses settle at night, making noises of all kinds; doors come open under the pressure of drafts. The dank, chill atmosphere was just the psychological effect of all those scary stories.

Then one summer Dalton's son, a brilliant man attending Oxford—with everything apparently going for him—went into the basement of the old house with a gun and blew his brains out. Not long after that Mr. Dalton himself suddenly dropped dead in his dressing room. Only one child remained, a daughter. She moved out at once. The magnificently renovated house was boarded up and left empty. No one went near it now. Cold and grim, it stood alone in the field of hops. Did old Mr. Ferreby have his wish at last?

Haunted Souls

What causes a ghost to remain on earth? Some have a wrong to set right, while others appear to be waiting for someone to join them. The ghosts in these tales continue to haunt the place of their death, and show no sign of moving on.

Lady in Waiting

Before the Louisiana Purchase in 1803, the state of Mississippi was part of the land owned by Spain and governed by Don Jose.

The governor's residence at Cottage Gardens in Natchez was a magnificent white mansion, surrounded by catalpa trees and magnolias. Near the end of the eighteenth century, Don Jose sailed to Spain and returned with a beautiful bride.

During the next two years, the happy couple held many parties at the estate. The lovely señora made friends quickly and was admired by all who visited Cottage Gardens.

The pleasant life in Natchez was soon interrupted by a devastating yellow-fever epidemic that took hundreds of lives. Even Don Jose's young bride

could not escape the indiscriminate malady. No medicine was available to ease the suffering, and victims were buried quickly to help contain the disease.

When stricken, she begged him to bury her on the bluffs overlooking the Mississippi River, which she had come to love during her brief time in the new country.

Don Jose granted her last request and then moved across the river, away from the deadly pestilence. Each evening he would stare at her small vault on the cliff and pray for her soul.

The enchanting señora, however, was not ready to leave Cottage Gardens. After the plague took her life, the stately mansion continued to be her spiritual residence.

During the Civil War, she was seen by soldiers settled at Natchez. Sentries who saw her said she was a beautiful woman who refused to obey their orders to stop and identify herself. Instead, the wispy phantom glided silently across the lawn as guard dogs cowered in fear between the soldiers' trembling legs.

Her small, delicate figure has been seen strolling through the magnolias for centuries. She is usually accompanied by the faint sound of a Spanish guitar, playing a haunting romantic melody. Perhaps Don Jose has also returned to Cottage Gardens to share in spirit the lovely wife he was denied in life.

Specter in the Court

On a hot summer afternoon, the grounds of the Old Penitentiary Building in the Washington Arsenal Prison were the last thing four prisoners saw before the hangman's noose ended their lives. The quartet were conspirators who had met with John Wilkes Booth to assassinate President Abraham Lincoln in 1865.

Those on the gallows were Mary Surratt, whose boardinghouse had served as the meeting place for Booth; Lewis Payne; George Atzerodt; and David Herold.

Mary Surratt claimed she was innocent and had played no role in the president's death. She insisted she didn't know her house was being used to plan the infamous deed.

A public outcry broke out over the decision to execute Mary Surratt, and several efforts were made

to save her. The court that found her guilty may have had some doubts, because it submitted a petition to President Andrew Johnson, asking that she be committed to prison for life.

Mary Surratt believed she would be spared, right up to the moment a white hood was placed over her head. But the executioner received no final reprieve, and Mary dropped through the trapdoor into eternity along with the others on that sweltering Friday afternoon.

The Washington Arsenal Prison was later changed into an army fort, and the courthouse where the conspirators were tried became an apartment in a section reserved for officers. All the tenants who have lived there have experienced the eerie presence of Mary Surratt.

Those who have seen her say the apparition is of a stout, middle-aged woman, who is dressed in black and seemingly glides above the floor.

In 1977, a lieutenant and his neighbor saw her moving along the corridor. Other families have been awakened in the middle of the night to hear strange sounds like murmuring voices.

On another occasion, a young officer was standing in the hallway and thought he saw his wife go into the bathroom. When he entered the bedroom, he was surprised to see her sleeping peacefully.

It is not known why the ghosts of the others who were hanged on July 7, 1865, never haunted the scene of their last hours on earth.

No one can explain why the spirit of Mary Surratt has returned from the grave—unless her ethereal wanderings are a sign that she is still determined to prove her innocence.

The Ghost with the Flaming Fingers

Every small town along the Hudson Valley in New York State has a pet ghost. Take, for instance, the famous ghost said to have been seen near Leeds, a few miles northwest of Catskill. She was a novel ghost for several reasons.

In the late 1700s, an unpleasant character named Ralph Sutherland came to this country from Scotland, bringing a servant girl with him. He was cruel to the young woman to the point where she could not stand it, and ran away.

Sutherland's anger knew no bounds. He mounted his horse and overtook her as she fled down a country road. Then he tied her hands together and, leaping upon his horse, dragged her back to the

house. Some said he tied her to the horse's tail. In any case, she was dead when they arrived home.

Sutherland was arrested and tried. He claimed that he had not meant to harm the girl, only to teach her a lesson. The horse had become frightened and had run away, he said, throwing him and dragging her to her death.

Sutherland's death sentence was suspended until he should reach 99 years of age, if he lived that long. In the meantime he was to wear a hangman's noose about his neck and report to the judges at

Catskill once a year. This, it is reported, he did. But in the meantime the ghost of the young girl began to haunt the area. She was seen sitting on the stone wall of the Sutherland garden with flames rising from each fingertip as she laughed long and loudly at the fear she aroused in the vicinity. At other times she was said to have been seen tied to a black horse's tail as it dragged her shrieking past Sutherland's house night after night.

But here the legend becomes confused. An almost identical account of the ghost of Leeds has the villain's name as Bill Salisbury, and the girl as a Native American sent to him as a servant by parents who couldn't control her. Furthermore, Salisbury was supposed to be hanged at 90 instead of 99, and instead of a noose he had to wear a red string around his neck.

This legend has the girl sitting on a rock—Spook Rock, it's called—with a lighted candle on each fingertip instead of flames, and a shaggy white dog howling, heartbroken, at her feet.

The Irish Apparition

On May 27, 1913, Lieutenant Desmond L. Arthur was returning to the airfield at Montrose, Scotland, after a routine flight. Without any warning his BE-2 folded like a broken kite 4,000 feet over the base and slammed into the ground. The dark-haired Irishman was killed instantly.

Training accidents in the Royal Flying Corps were not uncommon during those early days of aviation, but there was something unusual about this crash. As the fragile biplane descended for a landing, a wing strut snapped and flew into the air. All lift and control ceased and the stricken fighter plummeted quickly.

An official board of investigation studied the wreckage and discovered that the strut had failed due to faulty repair work. The accident report was

filed and the busy maintenance department was ordered to check wing struts more frequently for fatigue and stress. Case closed.

During the next three years, hundreds of students earned their wings at Montrose and some became aces during dogfights with the Imperial German Air Force in World War I.

In the fall of 1916, Major Cyril Foggin was walking

to the mess hall for dinner when he noticed another officer in flying gear ahead of him. The stranger continued toward the mess hall, reached for the door, and vanished. For a moment, Major Foggin thought he had imagined the incident, but the youthful fighter pilot had been a solid image.

A few days later, it happened again. Just as Foggin arrived at the mess hall, the silent flier appeared, marched right up to the door, and disappeared.

Major Foggin was not a fearful man. He had often faced death in the unfriendly skies over Germany. But the strange specter at the mess hall made his blood run cold. He decided to check with the flight surgeon until he learned that his colleagues had also seen the phantom airman.

Then the ghost began to appear at other locations on the airfield and became the subject of many heated conversations among the pilots.

One instructor was awakened one morning and stared across the room. Seated in a chair was a pilot dressed in a flight suit. "Who are you?" demanded the angry instructor. "What are you doing in my room?"

There was no response. When the instructor got out of bed and started across the floor, the uninvited visitor faded into thin air.

No one could understand why the ghost of Lieutenant Desmond Arthur was appearing at Montrose Airfield. When the anxious pilots reviewed the accident report regarding Arthur's crash, they were astounded to learn that the investigation board's original conclusion had been altered.

For some reason, the revised ruling blamed the accident on the unfortunate pilot rather than on incompetent maintenance.

Lieutenant Arthur's reputation as an excellent pilot had been tarnished, and his fellow airmen believed the board's slanderous statements caused him to return and defend his honor.

The spirit of Desmond L. Arthur continued to make ethereal appearances until Montrose Airfield was closed in 1963.

Famous Ghosts

E ven in the world of apparitions, stars can make their mark. Some of the people who were famous in life have returned to claim a new kind of recognition as ghosts. Here are some stories of those who have done just that. Is the limelight so hard to give up?

Washington Irving Returns

Libraries are wonderful storehouses for books offering adventure, romance, and mystery. The Astor Library in New York also offers a famous ghost.

In 1860, Dr. J. G. Cogswell was working there late one evening when he heard a sound a few aisles away. He got up, walked around a bookcase, and saw an old man reading at a table. The stranger looked familiar but Cogswell could not identify him in the sparse lighting. As he approached the shadowy figure, he realized he was looking at his old friend Washington Irving, who had written more than a dozen literary classics. There was only one thing wrong. Washington Irving had been dead for several months! Cogswell had been a pallbearer at Irving's funeral.

As Cogswell began walking toward his friend, the ghostly figure vanished. A few nights later, Cogswell was again working alone in the library when he saw his dead friend hunched over a book. The glowing white-haired phantom seemed oblivious to Cogswell and disappeared before the doctor could speak.

Cogswell finally told his friends about the supernatural visit, and was advised to spend a few days relaxing in the country.

But he was not the only person to see the famous author.

Pierre Irving, the writer's nephew, saw his uncle at the family residence in Tarrytown, New York. The apparition appeared in the parlor and walked to the room where Washington Irving had created *Rip Van Winkle* and other masterpieces.

Pierre stared quietly at his uncle's spirit. He was as shocked as Ichabod Crane meeting the Headless Horseman. Moments later, the hazy image faded away.

Ironically, the author of *The Legend of Sleepy Hollow*—America's first ghost story—did not believe in the supernatural. He would probably be amused to learn that he would become the most celebrated ghost in New York.

Not Gone with the Wind

One magnificent mansion in Atlanta is among the few antebellum homes to escape the disastrous fire during the Civil War. It was unharmed by General William Sherman as he marched through Georgia in 1864.

The stately house was built on 300 acres of woodland five years before the first shot was fired at Fort Sumter in April 1861.

Many ghosts have dropped in on this house, but the most famous visitor is the author whose epic novel about the Old South became a classic motion picture in 1939.

The spirit of Margaret Mitchell first appeared in the spring, several years after she sold the house. She had intended to help the new owner restore the

antique but died when she was hit by a car in 1946.

Margaret Mitchell had wanted to preserve the elegant estate that served as a model for Tara in *Gone with the Wind*.

On her first ethereal visit "she came through the closed door," said the owner. "Now she comes every year, carrying flowers and wearing a green dress. She never speaks. Instead, she always has an armful of jonquils as she wanders through the house."

After the first time the owner saw the famous author's ghost, he went to visit her grave. Her plot was covered by a bed of jonquils. Perhaps she wants to remain in the house that in life was so dear to her heart.

Custer Still Stands

George Armstrong Custer was a vain young man who seemed destined for a life of obscurity. Last in his class, but first in demerits, he barely managed to graduate from West Point.

Then fate opened a door and the failed student's leadership earned him a promotion to brevet major general during the Civil War. Custer's heroic tactics were inspiring as he galloped to glory from Bull Run to Appomattox. One decade later, the former class jester became a legend after the most famous battle of the Old West.

When the war ended, George Custer assumed his permanent rank of lieutenant colonel and took command of the Seventh Cavalry. The unit moved to Fort Abraham Lincoln, near Bismarck, in the Dakota Territory in 1873.

Three years later, the dashing young officer lost the only battle of his career—along with his life—during a brief skirmish with Sitting Bull at the Little Bighorn River. Hopelessly outnumbered by Sioux and Cheyenne warriors, the 36-year-old leader ordered an attack that would seal his fate.

In the fall of 1956, the famous battle was replayed to a couple on vacation. While exploring the battlefield, they came to a small hill and were surprised by a thrilling scene. Below the mountain were dozens of soldiers sitting on their horses, wearing tattered uniforms. They were covered with dried blood, crusted like black paint on their wounds. The astonished couple believed they were watching a Hollywood film crew making a war movie—until the troopers suddenly began to fade away.

A park ranger told the confused tourists they had seen the ghosts of the Seventh Cavalry. They had not been the first to report the phantom regiment.

Others have seen the restless spirits of Indian warriors who participated in the battle of the Little Bighorn.

They have been seen wearing warpaint and feathers in their headbands and carrying bows and arrows as their horses glide soundlessly across the grassy fields.

The ghosts of several officers assigned to Custer have also been seen over the years—especially that of Lieutenant Benjamin H. Hodgson, who was involved in a desperate battle several miles away from Custer's fateful last stand.

Although the legendary yellow-haired leader did not survive the furious conflict that bright Sunday morning, he now roams the battlefield, seeking his fallen comrades.

Another tourist, William Bell, met the famous commander at the Little Bighorn River. As Bell admired the lonely landscape, he noticed someone approaching. The man had long blond hair and was dressed in a buckskin coat. Bell instantly recognized George Custer, who seemed calm yet confused as he said, "Have you seen the Seventh? Where is the Seventh?" The specter glanced quizzically at Bell for a few moments, then vanished.

Custer's wife, Libby, knew her husband would not come back when the 7th Cavalry departed Fort Lincoln on May 17, 1876. As the band played "Garry Owen," a favorite of George Custer's, the morning sun's effect on the foggy clouds revealed an eerie scene of a ghostly regiment marching to its destiny.

Lost Over the English Channel

On a cold, rainy afternoon near Bedford, England, a small airplane took off and climbed into an overcast sky en route to Paris. The single-engine plane's two passengers were an army colonel and a musician. Moments later the plane slipped into the clouds.

It was never seen again.

When news of Glenn Miller's disappearance hit the papers, it momentarily stilled the hearts of all people who loved popular music. One of the world's most successful bandleaders had become another victim of World War II, which had already taken so many soldiers who had marched away to the sound of his music.

It was in Passaic, New Jersey, in 1942, that Glenn Miller announced he was disbanding his orchestra and joining the army. Many fans, and others in the music business, believe this decision marked the beginning of the end for big bands.

On December 4, 1942, the ex-civilian became Captain Glenn Miller and launched plans to modernize military music for the Army Air Forces.

The idea was not music to the ears of his superior officers. Miller was soon running a challenging obstacle course, designed by conservative, tone-deaf generals opposed to change. After more than a year of heated confrontations, the army brass surrendered reluctantly.

In 1943, Miller's innovative military band was heard on a weekly radio show throughout the CBS network, and it also recorded programs that were sent to the troops. Miller's most ambitious project was to take the band to Europe to entertain servicemen with special concerts, but the top brass erected another obstacle course.

Eventually, after nearly a year of badgering the War Department, Miller received orders to take his band to England in June 1944.

During the next five and a half months, Glenn Miller's Army Air Force Band thrilled thousands of servicemen at 71 concerts.

Miller was promoted to major on August 17, 1944, and began planning a Christmas concert for the troops in Paris.

Miller was scheduled to fly to Paris on December 14, but bad weather postponed the flight. He received a call from Colonel Norman Baesell, who was flying there the next day in the general's personal plane. Baesell invited Miller to join him.

That night Miller had dinner with his executive officer, Lieutenant Don Haynes, at the Officers' Club in Bedford, England. Haynes had been Miller's personal manager in civilian life, and the two men spent the evening discussing plans for a postwar band.

The weather was still dreary the next morning, but the forecast called for clearing in the afternoon. Miller and Haynes spent the morning eating breakfast and reading the newspaper. Then they drove to Twinwood Farm, 50 miles northwest of London. The plane was en route from another air station.

Miller was uneasy about flying and appeared very nervous as they waited in the staff car. The rain had become a steady drizzle, and he wondered if the pilot would be able to find them beneath the thick overcast.

Suddenly they heard a plane. The ceiling was about two hundred feet with poor visibility, but Flight Officer John Morgan was an experienced instrument pilot. The single-engine Norseman broke through the clouds, circled the field, and landed a few minutes later. Morgan taxied to the car, swung around and kept the engine running.

Miller and Baesell tossed their baggage into the plane and then climbed aboard. While buckling their seat belts, Miller said, "Hey, where are the parachutes?"

"What's the matter, Miller?" said Baesell. "Do you want to live forever?"

At 1:55 PM, Flight Officer Morgan released the brakes, began moving rapidly down the runway and was soon airborne. Less than a minute later the Norseman was swallowed by clouds.

Surprisingly, Glenn Miller's plane was not reported missing until Christmas Eve, nine days after it vanished.

Army officials believe the Norseman had been disabled by ice and crashed into the English Channel. Others disagree, and believe Miller's plane may have gone down over land. One who shares the latter theory is Dixie Clark, a radio operator at Twinwood Farm.

Shortly after takeoff, Flight Officer Morgan failed to respond to radio transmissions. Dixie Clark called several times but got no answer. She is certain the plane never made it to the Channel.

Glenn Miller had many friends and fans who were upset by the army's apparent indifference to his disappearance. They could not understand why a full-scale search was not launched when his plane did not land in Paris.

One reason was the Battle of the Bulge, a vital military operation that began on December 15—one day after Miller left England. Authorities were concentrating on blocking Germany's last major advance through the Ardennes in Belgium. They were not concerned about one overdue airplane when planes failed to return every day during the war. There wasn't time to search for them. Pilots and planes were desperately needed for combat and could not be spared for rescue missions.

An unusual incident occurred two days after Miller departed for Paris. Military policemen went to the Mount Royal Hotel, collected all of his belongings, and drove away. Allen Stillwell, Miller's personal valet, thought this was very odd since his boss had not yet been officially declared dead or missing. When Stillwell asked why the items were being boxed, the men said everything was being sent to his family. But his family never received any of Miller's clothes or personal effects.

The C64 Norseman that took Glenn Miller to an unknown destination was capable of making the flight that fateful Friday afternoon. The single-engine transport, used as a cargo and passenger plane during the war, could carry nine people at 148 miles per hour. It had no de-icing equipment, however, and many theorists believe that caused it to crash into the English Channel. Meteorologists, however, said icing conditions did not exist before or after the plane departed Twinwood Farm.

Flight Officer Morgan, a veteran of 32 combat missions in B-24 bombers, had spent one hour flying on instruments in thick clouds before picking up Miller and Baesell. He would never have flown a small plane anywhere that day if the weathermen had forecast icing at any altitude along his route to Twinwood Farm or Paris.

Icing is not the sole culprit responsible for aircraft disasters, yet it was the army's only explanation for the doomed plane. Investigators never considered engine failure as a probable cause.

If the Norseman had crashed before reaching the Channel, it seems likely that someone would have found it by now. During the Battle of Britain, the rugged hills and farmlands became a graveyard for scores of Allied and Axis aircraft. Since the war, an army of collectors roam the sites daily looking for wrecks and artifacts.

The fate of Glenn Miller may never be known, yet the famous bandleader may have unwittingly predicted his epitaph a few weeks before his final journey.

In a letter to his brother, Miller said, "By the time you receive this, we shall all be in Paris, barring of course a nosedive into the Channel."

A t some point in time everyone has experienced a sense of déjà vu, the feeling that they are reliving an event that has already occurred. But most people don't experience events that have yet to happen. Here are a few stories about people who were given glimpses of the future before returning to the present.

Vision of Doom

The sleeping mind may provide a unique theater that offers a dramatic story of a future event. Many people have had unusual experiences that coincided with visions from a prophetic dream. But it is extremely rare when two people share the same warning.

On May 11, 1812, Prime Minister Spencer Perceval of England told his family about a peculiar vision he had during the previous evening. Perceval was walking through the lobby of the House of Commons when he was confronted by a crazy man waving a pistol. The unfamiliar attacker, wearing a green coat with brass buttons, aimed the weapon at the prime minister and fired one shot. Then everything went dark and Perceval assumed that he must have died.

The haunting vision had been so clear, he was convinced it was an omen.

Surprisingly, a wealthy merchant named John
Williams had the same vision about Spencer
Perceval seven nights earlier. Williams had no interest in politics, but on May 4 he dreamed he was in
the cloakroom of the House of Commons and witnessed a shocking event. He saw a small man pull a

pistol from the pocket of his green coat and shoot the prime minister in the chest.

Williams awoke in a sweat and explained the nightmare to his wife, who showed little interest in having her sleep disturbed to listen to a ridiculous dream.

Williams was so distressed that he discussed the strange vision with his friends the next day. He considered calling the prime minister but changed his mind when they discouraged him from being so foolish.

On the morning of May 11, Spencer Perceval ate breakfast with his family. Although they did not really believe in dreams of doom, they urged him to stay home. He ignored their advice and said his presence was required at the day's session.

As Spencer Perceval strolled through the lobby of the House of Commons, a bushy-haired man stepped from behind a pillar and shot him to death. The crazed assassin was wearing a dark green coat with shiny brass buttons.

Preview to Disaster

In 1932, newspaper reporter J. Bernard Hutton and photographer Joachim Brandt were assigned to do a feature story on the Hamburg, Germany, shipyard.

They drove to the huge complex, interviewed several executives and workers, and completed the assignment by late afternoon.

As they were leaving, the two newsmen heard the unmistakable drone of aircraft engines and looked up to see the sky filled with warplanes. Then they heard the city's antiaircraft batteries opening fire as bombs began exploding around them.

Moments later, the area was a raging inferno as fuel tanks were hit. Warehouses were collapsing from high explosives and dock cranes were twisted into pretzels.

Hutton and Brandt realized this was no drill. They

rushed to their car as antiaircraft gunners began scoring hits on the bomber formation overhead.

At the gate, Hutton asked a security guard if there was anything they could do to help but was told to leave the area immediately.

Hutton and Brandt were confused when they drove into Hamburg. The sky had turned dark dur-

ing the attack, but now it was clear and the city was serene. The busy streets were not indented with craters and the buildings were intact. No one seemed concerned as they went about their daily business.

Hutton and Brandt stopped the car and looked back toward the shipyard. Now they received another shock because they saw no black ribbons of smoke rising into the sky and no damaged buildings. What was happening?

Back at the newspaper office, Brandt's pictures were developed and the two men got another surprise. Brandt had continued shooting film throughout the air raid, but his photographs showed nothing unusual. The shipyard looked as it did upon their arrival that morning. There was no evidence that a rain of bombs from enemy planes had destroyed the area, as they had witnessed.

The editor studied the photographs and wondered why Hutton and Brandt insisted they had been involved in an air attack. He dismissed their story and decided that they had probably stopped at a tavern for a couple of drinks on the way back to the office.

Just before World War II began, Bernard Hutton moved to London. In 1943, he saw a newspaper story about a successful raid by a Royal Air Force squadron on the Hamburg shipyard. He felt a cold shiver along his spine as he studied the photos. The scene of destruction was exactly as it appeared during his visit with Brandt in the spring of 1932.

There was only one thing different: Hutton and Brandt had witnessed the event 11 years before it happened.

Shake, Rattle, and Rock

The present is our only source of reality. Tomorrow has not happened and the past is history. Yet there are those who can transcend reality. The ability always involves an involuntary sensation that previews a particular event.

What special power allows certain people to slip through the veil of time and foresee images of future events? Somewhere between the fathomless mysteries of prophecy and prediction lies the phenomenon of premonition. Nearly everyone has had an eerie feeling that they will receive a phone call from a friend, or that a family member has been injured in an accident. Occasionally, someone will suddenly be stricken with visions of disaster. Although the sensation is clear and frightening, the person rarely knows when the calamity will occur.

At the turn of the century, San Francisco was booming, along with the rest of the nation. A decade of prosperity had followed the 1890s depression and the magnificent city was riding atop the boom. Its cheerful citizens were enjoying the promise of good times as they began the twentieth century.

Gerald Perkins was among the ambitious citizens enjoying a wave of optimism. Although his position as a bellman at the Fairmont Hotel was modest, he had visions of being promoted to management in the future.

On the afternoon of April 17, 1906, he had another vision.

Gerald Perkins had never had a premonition in his life but couldn't shake the bizarre image of impending disaster. For no apparent reason he pictured the city falling on him, followed by a raging firestorm that burned San Francisco to ashes.

The young man was confused but felt it was his moral duty to warn the guests of the frightening configuration. Perkins's supervisor, however, did not approve of the bellman alarming the patrons.

"What's the matter with you, young man?" cried the hotel manager. "We can't stay in business if you keep chasing people away with crazy stories."

"I can't explain it, sir," Perkins said. "It may not even happen. But can we take the chance and not warn everyone?"

"Warn them about what?" The manager was clearly worried, not about Perkins's vision but the possibility of losing customers. "Will telling everybody the world's going to end make them safe? You aren't setting a good example for the other employees."

Gerald Perkins's sensations grew stronger as he went about his duties. He refused to remain silent and was fired at the end of his shift.

He left the hotel and walked the streets, disturbed by his haunting premonition, as well as the prospect of looking for another job.

At 5:13 the following morning, there was a deep

rumbling, then a deafening roar that shook the proud city to death. During the next 65 seconds, streets rolled like ocean waves and tall buildings crumbled, while the sky rained tons of stone and glass. When the earth stopped shaking, the greatest city of the West was gone.

Gerald Perkins's deadly vision had become reality.

View of the Future

Victor Goddard was in serious trouble. The 37-year-old Royal Air Force pilot had been on a reconnaissance flight over Scotland. As he headed back to the air base, he flew into the heart of a vicious storm. While dodging broiling cumulus clouds, he was unable to see prominent landmarks. Soon he was lost.

It was 1934 and Goddard's Hawker Hart biplane did not have the sophisticated electronic navigational aids that would serve so well in the future. He caught brief glimpses of the mist-shrouded terrain while flying between cloud layers, but he could not determine his position.

Somewhere ahead was Drem, an abandoned RAF airfield. If he could find it, he could calculate a

new course home. Now, however, he was having difficulty just seeing through his rainswept goggles in
the open-cockpit plane. Goddard was worried that

his fragile craft might be ripped to shreds by the violent winds that were tossing him around the sky like a toy kite.

When his instincts told him he was nearing the deserted airfield, an incredible thing happened.

"Suddenly," he said later, "the area was bathed in an ethereal light, as though the sun were shining on a midsummer day."

Goddard eased back on the power and slipped downward around the towering clouds.

Then he saw it. Drem was just ahead.

As he approached the field, however, he wondered if he was in the right place. The airfield below as not deserted. It was alive with intense activity. As mechanics worked on a line of training planes, linemen were fueling other planes on the concrete tarmac.

Descending to 50 feet, the anxious pilot watched a group of cadets and instructors walking towards tows of yellow airplanes, parked on the ramp outside the huge hangars.

Victor Goddard's head was swimming with questions as he surveyed the unexpected scene. Why were the planes painted yellow? All trainers for the Royal Air Force were silver. And when had Drem been reactivated?

Finally, Goddard recognized familiar landmarks in the area and turned his Hawker Hart to a course that would take him home.

When he landed, he told his story, but no one believed it. His fellow airmen felt he had experienced a hallucination after being tossed around by the thunderstorm.

Four years would pass before Goddard learned the truth of what happened during that afternoon flight.

In 1934, Drem *was* an abandoned airfield whose hangars had almost collapsed. The runways and ramp areas were scarred with jagged holes and weeds.

But in 1938, as the ominous threat of war with Germany became a reality, Drem was reopened and rebuilt to train young men as fighter pilots. At that time, the color of the planes was changed from silver to yellow.

Goddard believed that when he descended below the clouds that stormy day in 1934, he slipped through a hole in time and flew four years into the future.

The Sorrowful Painting

Gilbert Charles Stuart's paintings are admired throughout the world. In 1777, his work was exhibited successfully at the Royal Academy and his *Portrait of a Gentlemen Skating* won special awards five years later.

He was ranked among the leading portrait artists in England. His paintings of America's prominent statesmen, such as George Washington, Thomas Jefferson, James Madison, and James Monroe, are excellent examples of his genius during a distinguished career.

One painting proved to be a portrait of tragedy.

The renowned artist was commissioned by Lord Mulgrave to do a painting of his brother, General Phipps. The army officer was soon to be posted to duty in India and would be away from home for a long time. Lord Mulgrave wanted a portrait of his

brother to display with other family members in the library during his absence.

Gilbert Stuart was a close friend of both men and wanted to please them with a portrait that would display General Phipps's finest qualities.

When the painting was unveiled, Lord Mulgrave gasped and nearly fainted from shock. Something was terribly wrong.

"Good God!" Lord Mulgrave cried. The horrible image on the canvas could not possibly be a reflection of his brother's persona. He regained his composure, stared at his friend in disbelief and wondered about the painting's sinister implications.

"What is this supposed to be?" Lord Mulgrave asked, pointing at the artistic monstrosity.

Gilbert Stuart was embarrassed, unable to explain his interpretation. He slowly shook his head, his eyes reflecting genuine regret.

"I simply painted what I saw in your brother's expression during our sessions together."

"But this is not my brother," insisted Lord Mulgrave. "This is the picture of an insane person."

Lord Mulgrave was so agitated that he refused to allow the portrait to be seen by anyone, including members of his family.

A few days later, General Phipps said good-bye and departed for his new assignment in India. Nothing more was heard for several months.

Then Lord Mulgrave received distressing news.

General Phipps was dead. Shortly after arriving in India, the eminent commander had committed suicide in a fit of insanity. Gilbert Stuart's prophetic painting became another eerie example of life imitating art.

Probably all of us, at one time or other, have encountered something that seemed out of sync. It might have been a vision of something that didn't belong—perhaps something in the wrong place at the wrong time. Here are a few curious tales of events that may have been off the time track.

Yesterday Is Today

On July 14, 1944, Royal Air Force pilot Thomas Clifford strafed a column of German tanks that were on their way to hammer Allied positions in Normandy. After several attacks, the 23-year-old squadron leader banked his Typhoon fighter away from the burning wreckage and headed back to his base.

North of Amiens, he spotted two planes that seemed to be engaged in a dogfight. As he flew closer, he identified one as an ancient SE5 biplane, used by the British during World War I. The pilot was in trouble, trying to control the plane as smoke streamed from the damaged engine.

Then Clifford noticed the plane that had attacked the SE5 and was astonished to see that it too was from World War I, a Luftwaffe triplane with large black Maltese crosses on the wings and fuselage.

He watched the German fighter close in on the SE5 for the kill and decided to participate. Clifford fired one burst from his guns and the tracers sliced into the archaic Fokker but seemed to have no effect.

As the Fokker dived for safety in the clouds

below, the young squadron leader noticed a look of fear on the German pilot's face.

The British SE5 was still struggling to remain airborne, but the pilot waved from his open cockpit and rocked his wings in gratitude. Clifford returned the wave and watched the old warbird glide down to an emergency landing.

Upon returning to his base at Kent, Thomas Clifford reported damaging the German tank convoy and casually mentioned that he had also taken a few shots at an antique German Fokker. The report was filed and forgotten, and Clifford did not think about the encounter again until July 1972. The Royal Air Force was holding a reunion and Clifford was invited, along with other former officers who had fought in World War II.

At the party in London, Clifford was introduced to retired squadron leader George Campbell, a former pilot with the Royal Flying Corps. Clifford was honored to meet with the old warrior, who had earned the Distinguished Flying Cross during World War I.

As always happens at military reunions, the men exchanged war stories, and Clifford described the two obsolete planes he had met near Amiens while flying back to his base.

"The Germans were really desperate by 1944," Clifford said, "because they were using old Fokker triplanes for trainers. But that's not the only odd thing. The Fokker was actually attacking another old World War I plane I'm sure was a British SE5."

Most of the listeners dismissed the story with a wry smile, but George Campbell's face turned pale.

"Do you remember the date?" asked Campbell, after recovering his composure.

"Not after all these years," confessed Clifford. "But it must have happened in July. I remember that because my birthday is in July."

George Campbell stared at Clifford with tears in his eyes. "It was July 14, 1918. I was flying that SE5."

Now it was Clifford's turn to feel weak in the knees, as Campbell told him how he had been on combat patrol near Amiens when bullets from an enemy plane struck his engine. The attacker was a blue and white Fokker DR1 with three wings.

"I realized that the enemy pilot had the advantage," said Campbell, "and I was helpless as he came from behind to finish me off. Suddenly I saw a strange aircraft diving and firing at the Fokker. The German quickly broke off his attack and headed for the clouds below us."

Icy fingers were crawling up Clifford's back as he listened to Campbell's story. He raised his hand and said, "I can tell you what happened next. Your engine was on fire and you waved to the strange airplane as you went down."

"That's right," exclaimed Campbell. "I was able to land but found myself on the wrong side of the lines. I was captured and put in a POW camp."

George Campbell told his listeners about a visitor he had while he was a prisoner of war. It was the pilot who had downed his SE5, a German ace who talked about attacking Campbell's plane and wondered about the unfamiliar monoplane they had seen come out of nowhere. The ace told Campbell he was glad the end of the war was near, because "that airplane could blow both of us out of the sky."

Campbell's visitor was Lieutenant Hermann Göring, holder of the Blue Max. He had assumed command of Captain Manfred von Richthofen's squadron after the Red Baron was shot down on April 21.

"It's very strange," said Tom Clifford, as he reminisced about his unusual experience. "I guess I could have flown into a time warp that day and slipped twenty-six years into the past. Campbell was convinced that I saved his life by firing at the old Fokker."

Tunnel to the Past

This fantastic incident is rumored to have occurred recently on a mountainside "somewhere out West." The person who reported it to me was a skeptic from New Mexico who didn't believe it actually happened. But he had been assured it was true by the person who told it to him. And he found it intriguing....

It seems that an amateur mineral collector was on a trip West and enjoyed exploring old mine shafts or tunnels he spotted from the highway. His wife was used to these side trips. She usually knitted in their car wile he hunted for rocks for his collection.

On one trip, he spotted a dark opening in the side of a high ridge. Stopping the car, he took his collecting bag and geologist's hammer and started off. He entered the cave and was soon in the gloom of a walk-in tunnel, apparently an old mine shaft. The roof seemed solid, and there seemed to be no snakes about; so he cautiously walked deeper into the shaft. After some distance, he noticed light up ahead. He hurried on, surprised that there should be another entrance so soon.

Moving forward, he came to a fork in the tunnel. One passage was dark and the other filled with an odd light from up ahead. Having no flashlight with him, he decided to follow the lighter corridor. He

turned left into one of the most astonishing experiences a rock hound ever had. As the tunnel grew lighter, he saw a small opening before him about two feet wide and a foot high. He got to his knees and looked into it and saw a wide valley stretched out below.

Then he gaped. In the center of this valley was a wagon train in a defensive circle. From one side a great horde of mounted Native Americas were attacking, waving bows and arrows and spears and whooping loudly enough to make his blood run cold.

Of course, he thought he was viewing a set for a TV show or a movie and, after recovering from his initial shock, watched with disinterested fascination. But the slaughter became so realistic and the screams of the wounded so fearful that his interest soon turned to horror and then panic. He finally tore his eyes away from the sight and with his fingers in his ears raced back through the tunnel. He burst out of the shaft just as his wife was coming to find him.

He told her what he had seen, and she, in equal

panic, said he had been gone over an hour and she had become worried. She had brought a flashlight with her. Together they went back into the tunnel. They could find no fork in the corridor, only a dead end a few feet inside the opening. The fork just wasn't there.

Later, when they described the incident, local residents seemed quite excited, for in the valley just behind the ridge where the tunnel was, an entire wagon train of pioneers had been massacred by Indians many years before. Perhaps through the now-vanished tunnel to the past he had witnessed a reenactment of the actual scene. Perhaps it was just as well he came back to modern times when he did. A little longer might have been too late.

A Switch in Time

On a cloudy summer evening, Bill Johnstone and Ian Lacey were enjoying a bicycle ride through the Welsh hills. Near Rhondda Cynon Taff, a heavy rainstorm forced them to seek shelter at a nearby railway signal tower. They could not imagine the eerie adventure awaiting them. The date was July 15, 1945.

The two friends parked their bikes and hurried inside the small house, where they were welcomed by an aging signalman.

After removing their drenched capes, they warmed themselves near the glowing stove and watched the old man manipulate several switching levers.

Bill and Ian thought there was something odd about him. His uniform did not resemble any they had seen in recent years. As he went about his work, the signalman kept mumbling to himself, but the two friends could not understand his ramblings.

At 8:15 Bill and Ian heard a train approaching but couldn't see it through the rain-swept windows. As the train roared past the signal tower, the old man quickly began moving switching levers.

What happened next took both friends by surprise. Above the sound of the furious winds, they heard the unmistakable screech of metal wheels on railroad tracks, followed by a horrendous crash and the anguished screams of passengers.

Instantly, they rushed outside and ran toward the calamity which was momentarily hidden from view. When they reached the end of the platform, they could not believe their eyes.

There was no disaster—no buckled, shattered railroad cars; no smoking, damaged engine; and no passengers. Nothing but an endless expanse of rusted rails and weeds that stretched into the distant hills.

As they walked back to the signal tower, they noticed that it was dark and deserted. The door was broken, flapping like a flag in the wind. Inside, they found another shock. The small room was a maze of cobwebs, and the stove did not look as if it had held a fire for a long time. The dusty floor was covered with leaves and the switching levers were stiff with age.

Bill looked inside the stove and pulled out several newspapers that were nearly twenty years old.

The two friends rode their bikes to an inn about five miles from the mysterious signal box. There they learned that many villagers believed the old signal box was haunted by the ghost of Joshua Thomas, the man who was on duty when the 8:15 slammed into another train. Joshua had fallen asleep and then thrown the wrong switch when he heard the approaching express train. He was fired, found guilty, and hanged himself.

In their hotel room, Bill and Ian read the yellowed newspapers where the tragic story unfolded just as described at the inn.

One newspaper was dated December 4, 1927, and the headline read: TRAIN CRASH HORROR—16 DIE. Next they looked at another edition published after the official inquiry. It was dated July 12, 1928, and said: SIGNALMAN BLAMED FOR RAIL CRASH. The board members held that Joshua Thomas was solely responsible for the catastrophe. The saga ended with the July 16 edition, with a report that "Signalman Joshua Thomas was found hanged yesterday. . . ."

The photo of Joshua in the newspaper revealed the same man who had welcomed them into the signal box during the storm.

Bill and Ian were never able to find a reason for their unusual encounter. They only knew that when they walked into the signal box that stormy summer night at Cynon Gap, they stepped 18 years into the past.

Ten Minutes Late

On a calm, clear night in 1963, a National Airlines jetliner was cruising smoothly above the Atlantic Ocean. The crew aboard the Boeing 727 admired the sparkling lights of Florida's coastline ahead.

Shortly after contacting Miami Approach Control, the huge three-engine airliner disappeared. All attempts to contact the plane were in vain.

The astonished air traffic controllers couldn't imagine what had happened when the blip representing the plane vanished from their radar screens.

Miami Approach Control queried the crews of other planes flying in the same area as National's B-727. No one had seen a bright fireball signifying an explosion, and no reports were heard from a plane in distress.

Everything seemed to be routine in the moonlight skies over the Atlantic.

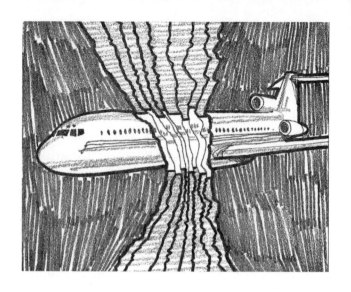

Then, ten minutes after the Boeing 727 disappeared from radar, it suddenly reappeared! And it reappeared in exactly the same location where it had vanished!

Anxious air traffic controllers made contact with the plane.

"How are you doing out there?"

"Everything's fine," said the captain. "It's a beautiful night."

The crew obviously didn't know they had been missing in time and space for ten minutes. The rest of the airliner's flight was normal. After landing at Miami International Airport, it taxied to the gate.

As the pilots shut down the engines, they were mildly surprised by the flashing lights of emergency vehicles approaching their plane. Officials began to question passengers as they came out the door.

"How do you feel?"

"Did you experience anything unusual during your flight?"

The unexpected inquisition from the excited mob of officials confused and upset many passengers. The flight had been smooth and enjoyable. The only thing weird in their minds was the silly questions from the crowd blocking their path to the gate.

When told that their plane had vanished from radar for ten minutes, the crew thought someone was playing a joke on them. Officials could not convince them they had ceased to exist during a ten-minute period of the flight, nor that the plane had suddenly reappeared on radar at the exact position it had disappeared.

"No matter what you say, Captain," said the airline's gate agent, "I'll need a deviation report because you were ten minutes late."

"That's nonsense," said the captain, looking at his watch. "What time do you have?"

That's when the pilots became believers.

The crew checked their watches against clocks on the ground. The time on all their watches, as well as the clocks in the cockpit, were exactly ten minutes slower than actual time.

Where did the airliner go when it vanished from the radar? Somehow, the plane managed to slip into another dimension for ten minutes, and no one aboard was ever aware of any change.

Massacre of the Cree

The storm had come up fast, and there had been no warning. If Denny had thought he'd have to deal with the torrential rains that he was fighting now, he never would have come out for this "relaxing" day of fishing and hunting.

The weather had looked perfect when he started out with an Indian guide, a packhorse, and a collapsible boat, in which he had decided to return while the Indian and the packhorse took the overland route. The day's sport had turned out to be great, but the boat was undoubtedly a mistake.

One of the original officers of the Northwest Mounted Police, Cecil A. Denny was stationed at Fort Walsh on the Oldman River in the part of the Northwest Territories that is now the Province of

Alberta in Canada. He knew that sudden wild storms like this were not uncommon.

Now, he practically lost the oars as the boat crashed against a particularly large stone. The frail boat was definitely not meant to function in these swirling rapids and whirlpools. It was getting battered and snagged on the rocky, shallow riverbed. It was only a matter of time before it would be completely destroyed.

On the left side of the river, he thought he could see a clump of trees through the relentless rain. He managed to get the boat to the bank of the river and dragged it up on the shore. As he ran ahead to get some shelter, he heard Indian drums rising above the thunder, and he heard chanting.

He moved through the trees, which unloaded another shower of water on him, and peered beyond them.

He saw a clearing in which there was an Indian camp. Beyond that some shaggy horses were grazing.

The peculiar thing was that neither the horses nor the people seemed to be paying any attention to the horrendous weather that was going on all around. The little children were playing out in the open as if no rain were coming down. The flaps to the teepees were open—and most of the Indians Denny knew feared thunder and usually drew the flaps of their tents closed at the first sign of a storm.

But that was all right, he thought. They were Cree. He could tell from the decorations on the teepees. The police had a good relationship with the Cree. He could probably get some food and maybe a chance to get dry.

That was when the lightning hit him, and he found himself flat on the ground, enveloped in a strange blue flame.

He lay unconscious for a few minutes, and then managed to get up and start for the camp. But it wasn't there. The tents, the people, the playing children, the horses were all gone.

He climbed a hill, expecting that from there he could see them traveling off, but there was no sign of them. Maybe he'd been unconscious for longer than he thought?

Denny knew it made no sense to try to get back to the fort by boat, so he began walking. He made it back, mostly by guesswork, by around midnight.

A few days passed, and as soon as he could get away, he went back to pick up the boat he'd abandoned along the upper reaches of the Oldman River. The Indian guide and the packhorse went with him.

When they finally found the boat, Denny and his guide carefully went over the ground where he had seen the Indians. There was no evidence that they had been there—only a few rings of stones, overgrown by grass; some bleached bones; and a couple of human skulls.

As they traveled back, the Indian guide told Denny that his grandfather had often talked about a terrible massacre of Cree Indians that had taken place at that very spot. The killers were a murderous bunch of Blackfoot Indians, the traditional enemy of the Cree.

It was a sneak attack, in which they killed every man, woman, and child, torched the teepees, and stole everything else. That had happened when his grandfather was a little boy.

Denny suddenly realized what he had seen. It was a reenactment of the day of the massacre. If he hadn't been struck by lightning, perhaps he might have witnessed the whole thing. That would explain why the people didn't notice the weather. They were experiencing the weather at a different time. He had heard of such ghostly reenactments of battles—in England, usually—when some kind of great or terrible event took place. But if it happened in England, it probably happened other places as well.

How many times, he wondered, in all the generations since the massacre had the cruel, barbaric attack been replayed? How many times would it act itself out again in the future?

There is something frightening about the sudden disappearance of people or things. One moment they are there, and the next they have vanished without a trace. There are tales of vanishing individuals, ships, planes— even whole towns. Here are a few of the most baffling.

Twenty Minutes from Home

A cheerful holiday spirit swept through Isla Grande Airport in San Juan, Puerto Rico, as passengers lingered at the Air Transport ticket counter. Most were remembering Christmas with relatives and friends only three days earlier. Now they were leaving the island and looking forward to celebrating New Year's in southern Florida.

As was the routine, Air Transport's agents checked reservation lists, slipped boarding passes into ticket folders, and courteously answered endless questions from the 27 passengers scheduled for the flight to Miami.

Outside, a ground crew prepared a DC-3 for the thousand-mile journey, and signed off NC-16002 as fueled and airworthy.

At 10:03 PM on December 28, 1948, Captain

Robert Linquist advanced the throttles and First Officer Ernest Hill called out the airspeed as the DC-3 rolled along Runway 27. Moments later, the twin-engine piston airliner was climbing into a clear sky. The 28-year-old captain was a former military aviator with 3,265 hours in his logbook and had flown the route many times.

In the cabin, stewardess Mary Burks attended to the passengers, including two infants. Everyone was in a festive mood and singing holiday carols as a tailwind gently pushed them toward the coast of Florida.

No one could know that fate would change the flight plan.

At 11:33 PM Captain Linquist called the Air Route Traffic Control Center in Miami and said they were cruising at 8,500 feet in clear skies. He estimated their arrival time at 4:05 AM.

At 4:13, Linquist and Hill could see the glowing lights of Florida's coastline. Hill told air traffic control they were 50 miles south of Miami and expected to land in 20 minutes.

No one ever heard from the DC-3 again.

When the plane failed to arrive, attempts to contact it were made by controllers in Miami, San Juan, and New Orleans. There was no reply.

Ninety minutes later, the Coast Guard knew the DC-3 was down somewhere. It would have used all its fuel by 5:45 AM.

A massive search began at sunrise as ships and aircraft swept the ocean from San Juan to Florida, covering the Caribbean, the Keys, the Bahamas, and the Gulf of Mexico. The water level was so shallow in the area where copilot Ernest Hill last spoke with controllers that objects could be seen clearly on the sandy bottom.

But no trace of the DC-3 was found. No twisted debris, no life jackets, no oil slick, and no sharks, that always appear at the scene of a disaster. Nothing but calm seas and sunny skies.

Something happened when the plane was only 20 minutes away from landing on that peaceful Tuesday morning. Something so swift that neither Captain Linquist nor First Officer Hill could report their dilemma to Miami.

Whatever it was will forever remain a mystery.

A Beautiful Day for Flying

The sunny skies offered a light easterly breeze as Andrew Carnegie Whitfield climbed into his silver and red monoplane at noon on April 15, 1938. Moments later the craft began rolling along the turf runway and was soon airborne.

Whitfield's airplane carried ten gallons of gas, which would allow him to fly for as long as three hours. He had told friends he was going to Brentwood and would return before sunset.

Andrew Whitfield, a nephew of billionaire philanthropist Andrew Carnegie, was proud of his private pilot's license. He had logged 200 hours, and was only 50 hours away from taking his flight test for a commercial license.

The 28-year-old Princeton graduate loved flying,

but never expressed any thoughts of becoming a professional aviator. He was content to "slip the surly bonds of earth" just for the fun of it.

Whitfield departed from Roosevelt Field on the same runway Charles Lindbergh used on his historic transatlantic flight. But Whitfield's destination was only 22 miles away across dry land.

Andrew Whitfield should have arrived at Brentwood Airport around 12:30, but he never landed there . . . or anywhere else.

An extensive five-day air and ground search yielded no clues. Scores of people combed every field where the missing flier might have made an emergency landing.

It seemed impossible that Whitfield's plane could vanish over a densely populated area. Yet, that's exactly what happened one sunny afternoon during a 30-minute flight over Long Island.

No one ever saw Andrew Whitfield again.

Flight 11 Is Missing—Again

On August 15, 1976, Flight 11 taxied away from the Saeta Airlines gate in Quito, Ecuador, and took off for a short journey to Cuenca. When the airliner was eight minutes away from its destination, the captain called the tower with his position and was cleared to land.

Flight 11 never arrived.

Extensive searches failed to find any trace of the four-engine Vickers Viscount and its 59 passengers.

The airline's president said, "It's possible the aircraft may have crashed, but it was only eight minutes away from Cuenca. And it's not possible to crash that close without detection."

Then, nearly three years later, it happened again.

Another Saeta Viscount, also designated Flight 11, departed Quito on April 23, 1979. The crew

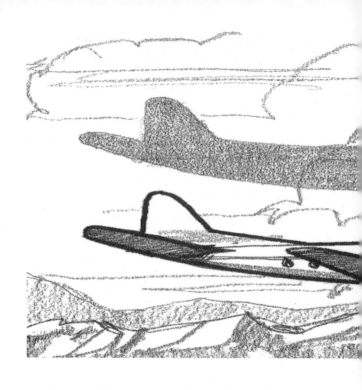

made a routine report to the Ambato relay station, and then vanished with 57 passengers.

After each airliner disappeared, massive air and

land searches were made by army patrols and planes from the Ecuadorian and American air forces.

In both incidents weather conditions were excellent,

and each plane had been in contact with the Ambato relay station. During the flight involving the second Viscount, the captain was called on the company frequency by another plane that requested a weather report. Captain Eduin Alexandre said, "The sky is beautiful and everything's fine."

Those were his last words.

If either Viscount had experienced an in-flight emergency, one of those pilots could have called the Ambato relay station. Whatever happened must have occurred so swiftly that neither crew had time to report the problem.

Investigators admitted they could not explain how two large turboprop airliners could vanish over land on a 45 minute flight in good weather.

Although a substantial reward was offered by the Ecuadorian government, Saeta Airlines, and grieving families, the fate of the 116 passengers has never been determined.

Missing Crew

The crews of ships and airplanes have to follow very specific orders, but what happens when they deviate from these orders? What could compel a crew to abandon ship or a pilot to unexpectedly land a plane without providing an explanation? Here are some stories of people who did just this—and were never heard from again.

Emergency Landing

After a bombing mission on November 23, 1944, a B-17 Flying Fortress with a ten-man crew was struggling to remain aloft with only two of its four engines running. The huge bomber was riddled with bullet holes, and flak had ripped away large sections of the fuselage.

As the B-17 approached a farmer's field in Belgium, a British antiaircraft crew looked up to see the plane descending for a landing.

"It's one of them Forts," said a gunner. "He's coming right down where we are."

"His landing gear's down," said another man, "and he's got two engines stopped."

"He's crazy," said the leader. "This is a farm, not a bloody airport!"

They did not realize the pilot may have considered

the expansive field a perfect "airport" for an emergency landing.

The gunners scrambled behind their sandbags and watched the B-17 slowly descend during its approach, then land in the freshly plowed turf.

As the bomber rolled past them, one of the wheels buckled in the soft ground. The plane swung around violently and came to rest.

They waited for the crew to come tumbling out of the wounded plane and wondered why the pilots didn't shut down the two good engines. After a few more moments, two gunners went to the Flying Fortress. Anxiously, they looked in the Plexiglas windows and received a horrifying shock.

"There's no one in that thing!" shouted the gunner.

It was true. A closer inspection revealed that the entire crew was missing.

The chief gunner called his command post on the radio and reported what had happened. He gave the plane's identification number and insignia.

The report was passed up through channels until

it reached John Crisp, a British officer. Within 30 minutes he arrived at the scene and talked briefly to the gunners.

Crisp went to the B-17 and looked inside. He tried to open the front hatch but it was locked. The bomb bay doors were closed and secured. Every door on the giant bomber was locked from the inside. Crisp walked along the fuselage to the waist-gunner's position. He eased through the narrow opening, slid around the .50-caliber machine gun, and dropped to the deck. Everything appeared normal at each duty station as he made his way to the cockpit. He sat in the pilot's seat and shut down the two engines, shrouding the bomber in an eerie silence. All controls were set for a landing—flaps down and landing gear extended.

Crisp began an inspection that became more perplexing with every minute. He found the navigator's logbook and a document with classified radio call signs. Surprisingly, the supersecret Norden bombsight was intact and uncovered. Bombardiers always armed an explosive device on the Norden equipment before bailing out to prevent it from falling into enemy hands.

But the men had not abandoned the airplane as it flew home from the mission. Crisp found all the parachutes and fur-lined flight jackets, as well as several candy bars.

But he couldn't find a single crewman.

A complete report was sent to the operations officer of the Eighth Air Force in Brussels. An inspection team dispatched to examine the mystery came back shaking their heads. What happened to the crew? The two waist-gunners' positions were not large enough for a man to squeeze past the gun mount while wearing a bulky parachute. The inspectors wondered why anyone would want to exit the plane from those positions when they could easily jump from the hatches or bomb bay. The theories were academic because every parachute was still in the plane. No one had bailed out.

And there was the annoying problem of the controlled descent to a textbook landing.

The ten airmen were never seen again.

Forty Yards Across the Dunes

On July 24, 1924, two Royal Air Force pilots boarded their single-engine biplane and climbed into the sunny skies over the Mesopotamian desert. Arab hostilities had increased, prompting intelligence officers to schedule daily surveillance flights.

Lieutenant W. T. Day and Officer D. R. Stewart were flying the morning reconnaissance mission and should have returned in four hours.

The two young men were never seen again.

The operations officer realized something was wrong by the time he sent out the afternoon recon sortie.

Where were Day and Stewart?

When the dispatch calculated that the aircraft had exhausted its fuel supply, it was getting too dark to start looking for the overdue flight.

An aerial search began the following morning and the airplane was found quickly by the rescue team. But a four-day search by air and ground forces found no trace of the two RAF officers. Investigators were stumped, unable to understand why Day and Stewart had landed on the blistering sands.

The airplane was intact and told them a great

deal—with the exception of one critical piece of information: what had happened to its crew.

One discovery was bizarre. Day and Stewart had vanished 40 yards from their deserted aircraft. That's where the footprints ended in the sand. It looked as if the two airmen had been plucked from the desert by some mysterious force.

Someone suggested that the men had been captured by Arabs, but there were no signs of the struggle that would have taken place if Arabs had attacked the fliers. And the only footprints came from the boots worn by the two airmen.

Meteorologists at the base confirmed that no unusual weather conditions had existed that would have prevented Day and Stewart from continuing the flight. Skies were clear and visibility was unlimited.

The abandoned plane had no bullet holes that might have been the reason the men made an emergency landing. Investigators could find no oil from the engine streaking along the fuselage. All flight controls worked perfectly and there was sufficient fuel in the tanks. The engine started quickly, and the plane was flown back to the base.

The plane was not the problem. Something else had caused the two young men to land on the inhospitable sand dunes.

Flight Lieutenant Day and Pilot Officer Stewart must have seen something in the air or on the sun-bleached desert that made them terminate the flight, climb out of their plane and walk side by side for 40 yards. But what was it?

Odyssey of the L-8 Blimp

Lieutenant Ernest D. Cody and Ensign Charles E. Adams were in a cheerful mood that fateful Sunday morning as they manned an L-8 blimp at six o'clock. A gray overcast sky awaited them as they prepared for a routine antisubmarine patrol over San Francisco Bay.

The date was August 16, 1942.

Lieutenant Cody thought the blimp was too heavy with dew to be able to take off. In an attempt to reduce the blimp's weight, he excused a third member of the crew, Machinist's Mate James Hill, from the mission. Hill exited the blimp and returned to the barracks.

Although his patrol, designated Flight 101, was routine for 27-year-old Ernest Cody, it was momentous

for Charles Adams. After 15 years service as a machinist's mate, the 38-year-old sailor had just been commissioned, and this was his first flight as an officer.

Neither man realized it would be his last day on earth. During the next two hours, Cody and Adams searched for underwater shadows and oil slicks, indicating the possible presence of enemy submarines. Cruising about 300 feet above the water, Cody and Adams waved to crewmen aboard the fishing boats dotting the whitecaps and noticed a pair of coast guard and navy vessels routinely patrolling the area.

At about 7:50 AM, Cody spotted an ugly black scar marring the blue water. He alerted the base: "Am investigating suspicious oil slick. Stand by."

Fisherman aboard the small boats saw the blimp drop two smoke flares and feared that it was going to release a depth charge. All eyes were glued to the airship. But the blimp did not drop a bomb or even make another circling pass. The fishermen were astonished to see it soar rapidly upward and disappear.

Operations personnel at Moffett Field had not been able to contact the L-8 since Lieutenant Cody sent his last radio call at 7:50 AM. They were puzzled, but not alarmed, attributing Cody's silence to radio failure. After all, the weather was clear and both men were airship veterans who could handle an in-flight emergency.

When Cody failed to report at 9:30, Lieutenant Commander George F. Watson, commanding officer of Airship Squadron 32, sent an alert to all ships and aircraft in the area. Surely someone would see the elusive blimp over San Francisco Bay.

A pair of OS2U Kingfishers took off from Alameda Naval Air Station to join the search. At 10:20 a Pan American World Airways pilot spotted the airship. Ten minutes later it was seen by one of the Kingfisher pilots who said it seemed to be out of control. But before the pilot could get close enough to investigate, the L-8 descended into the overcast.

At 10:45 the Army Coast Artillery Station at Fort Funston called Moffett Operations. On a beach near the Olympic Club Lakeside golf course, two surf fishermen had seen the huge blimp coming right at them. They thought her crew must be in trouble, since both her engines had stopped and her propellers were windmilling silently.

When the airship touched down, they dropped their fishing poles and grabbed her tow lines in a futile effort to ground her. A glance through the gondola's windows revealed nothing amiss—except no one was aboard!

Strong winds had torn the lines from their hands and the blimp danced across the beach until it was blocked by a precipice. One of the depth charges fell harmlessly to the ground. Then, 300 pounds lighter, the L-8 had risen skyward and vanished over the cliff.

"Any news of the crew?" Watson asked quickly.

"Two men jumped off when she hit the beach," came the answer.

Commander Watson relaxed. At least the crew was safe. Then a puzzling thought: Why would Cody and Adams leave the blimp unattended? Both men knew the airship tradition of "staying with the ship." There was no indication that they had faced grave danger.

A phone call from the police chief in Daly City, a suburb of San Francisco, interrupted Watson's speculation. A blimp had landed on a residential street, severing telephone and electrical wires, colliding with several parked cars, and finally coming to rest against a utility pole. A search had failed to find any trace of the crew.

Watson joined the salvage crew at the crash site. A quick inspection revealed that the airship was in excellent condition, though its huge, deflated envelope had been slashed by firemen to see if anyone had been trapped inside.

Then Naval Intelligence presented Watson with a new mystery. After questioning personnel on all the fishing boats, they learned that Cody and Adams had not abandoned the L-8 while it was cruising over the bay, nor had they jumped to the ground when it landed on the beach. Apparently, the army had mistaken the two surf fishermen for the crew.

Now Watson really began worrying about Cody and Adams. Five hours had passed since their last message. How could they have disappeared from a blimp cruising over a channel crowded with boats?

An extensive search was begun by the Army, Navy, Coast Guard, and state highway patrolmen.

The salvage crew hauled the blimp to a hangar at Moffett, where an examination only deepened the mystery. Her gondola was spotless. Nothing was missing except the bright yellow life jackets worn by Cody and Adams. All parachutes, as well as the life raft, were properly stowed above the polished deck. The radio worked and was set to the proper frequencies. The confidential briefcase was secured. The airship's ignition switches were on and the Warner Super Scarab engines were operational.

Searchers swept the coastline for weeks, yet no sign of Cody and Adams could be found. What happened to Lieutenant Cody and Ensign Adams as they circled the bay in view of numerous witnesses?

One investigator suggested that an enemy submarine had surfaced and surprised the blimp. This idea was dismissed, because the sub would have been seen by fishermen as well as the crews of the Coast Guard and Navy vessels.

Another theory proposed that the airmen may have lost their balance and fallen out the door. But the two would have been seen falling into the sea. Besides, the captain of the *Daisy Gray* had seen both men in the L-8 as it cruised over the bay, and the gondola door had been closed.

Regardless of Lieutenant Cody's situation, it is inconceivable that he would not have radioed his problems and intentions to Moffett Field. But, apparently, there was no problem to report. The blimp had suffered no failure of its engines, flight controls, or communications equipment, and all emergency items were intact.

A board of investigation studied volumes of data and interviewed many witnesses. After analyzing the material and testimony, they were no closer to solving the mystery than when they started.

The disappearance of Lieutenant Ernest Cody and Ensign Charles Adams remains one of the most baffling mysteries of naval aviation.

Ship Without a Crew

In late February 1855, the *James B. Chester* was about 600 miles southwest of the Azores—an island group some 800 miles off the coast of Portugal—when she was spotted by a lookout on the British ship *Marathon*.

Deckhands watched curiously as the three-masted bark sailed closer, her white billowing sails set to keep the big ship sailing on course.

As the *James B. Chester* drew nearer, the British seamen noticed something that caused them to stare in disbelief. There was no helmsman at the wheel. In fact, no crewmen could be seen on deck or in the rigging. The mysterious vessel appeared to be a derelict.

On the *Marathon*, the master's thoughts suddenly shifted from the bark's unfortunate plight to thoughts of salvage rights.

A boarding party rowed to the strange vessel and

made a perplexing discovery. There was no one aboard.

A search above and belowdecks revealed that some unusual activity had occurred, but there were no signs of violence. Furniture was overturned, articles scattered in the cabins, drawers ransacked, yet there was no blood nor any indication of the struggle that would have taken place if the vessel had been attacked by pirates or seized by a mutinous crew.

And, an ill-fated victim of piracy or mutiny was usually scuttled to remove all evidence that could be used in a maritime court.

A cursory inspection revealed that the cargo was intact, along with the ship's stores and fresh water. All lifeboats were secured in their davits. Only the compass and logbook were missing.

The *James B. Chester* had sustained no damage from storms, fires, or explosions.

For some reason, the captain and crew had abandoned a vessel that was seaworthy in all respects. This gave rise to a new mystery: How did the crew leave the ship?

Seafaring Ghosts

T he seas are mysterious and strange worlds unto themselves. Many things happen on their shores, upon their surfaces, and beneath their waves that are difficult to explain away. The following mysteries of the deep are just a few that have never been solved.

Phantom of the Sea

Everyone loves a good mystery, a chilling tale that provides a passport to the unknown, offering amusement and escape from the daily stress of work and bumper-to-bumper traffic. Fanciful stories let us relax before turning out the light and falling asleep. But what happens when fantasy becomes reality?

On a crisp autumn morning in 1883, the *J. C. Cousins* took up a position outside the mouth of the Columbia River in Oregon. The 87-foot, two-masted schooner no longer sailed the seas as an elegant passenger ship. She had become a sullied lady, cruising back-alley river routes as an escort vessel. The waters of the Columbia were treacherous, and merchant ship captains demanded an experienced skipper to guide them across the sandbars.

On October 6, Captain Alonza Zeiber, master of

the *Cousins*, dropped anchor and began waiting for the arrival of a French bark that was due from Saigon the next day. He did not know this would be his last voyage.

Coast guardsmen in the Canby lighthouse watched the schooner throughout the night, and saw her heading for open sea the next morning.

Then the astonished men witnessed an incredible sight. They were unable to explain why the *J. C. Cousins* suddenly turned around and began sailing toward them. What was Captain Zeiber thinking? He was deliberately steering the schooner to certain doom.

Observers on the beach were shocked and felt a chill as they heard the crunching sound of the *Cousins*'s hull scraping the sandbar, then watched helplessly as huge waves pushed her deeper into the mire. Anxious seamen trained binoculars on the schooner but saw no distress rockets, no signal flags being hoisted, nor anyone abandoning ship.

Surfboats were sent to investigate with no response to frantic calls. The reason became obvious when the rescue team boarded the *Cousins*.

Captain Zeiber and his three-man crew had vanished.

The schooner's lifeboats were still in their davits and everything was normal—except for the absence of her crew. The last log entry, "All's well," was written by Alonza Zeiber shortly after sunrise.

Another odd discovery was made belowdecks. Rescuers found a fire in the galley stove and the morning meal untouched on the table. The crew's quarters revealed no signs of a disturbance that would have been made by men leaving the ship in haste.

There was no reason to explain why Captain Zeiber ran his ship into the sandbar. Perhaps the crew was no longer aboard when the *Cousins* came about and sailed toward the calamity. If that were true, what had caused the ship to swing around and head directly into danger, instead of drifting out to sea on the morning tide?

Investigators thought the schooner's steering gear might have failed, but they were more confused when the rudder and steering apparatus were found undamaged.

Sometime during that peaceful morning an unknown force seized command of the *J. C. Cousins* and took her crew to a destination not found on any chart.

Lost at Sea

Mike was a sport fisherman, in the market for a new boat. A friend gave him the name of a woman with a boat she was trying to unload. He told Mike that she was desperate, and he could get a good deal.

Mike went with the woman to a marina in Sheepshead Bay, Brooklyn, where he got a look at the boat. It was beautiful—a cabin cruiser, fully equipped and in perfect shape—a boat to dream about.

"I want to get rid of it. Just make me an offer," said the woman. That's how Mike picked up a $50,000 boat for $10,000.

After they signed the papers, the woman relaxed and began to talk. The boat had belonged to her husband, Wayne, and he had taken great care of it.

When they found it deserted, they knew Wayne had to be lost at sea. Nothing else could have gotten him away from the boat. But his body had never been found.

Mike moved the boat to his own dock in Coney Island. He took it out a couple of times, and soon he was sailing like an old pro.

It was late in the afternoon on a hot, sticky day in August when Mike, his cousin Alan, and another friend, Peter, went fishing. It wasn't a good day to go out. The sea was rough and fog was rolling in. Soon they had gone so far, they couldn't see the shore.

Mike turned off the engine and they sat there fishing and drinking beer. It got dark. They were telling stories, and the fog got thicker. Soon, it was pitch-black all around them and strangely quiet. They couldn't even hear the buoy bells.

About ten o'clock they figured they'd go back. Mike went to turn on the engine, but it wouldn't start. Then they tried to use the radio. It was jammed.

As they sat on the deck, trying to figure out what

to do next, the cabin and deck lights went out. They were in what seemed like complete darkness.

They started blaming each other, fighting. Then Mike mentioned that the boat's previous owner had been lost at sea.

"Maybe it's that guy Wayne's fault," Mike said. "He probably doesn't want anyone else sailing his boat."

"No," said Alan, "he's a good guy. Look at what good care he took of it."

Finally, sometime after midnight, they decided to go to sleep in the cabin and just wait for daylight.

The next thing Mike knew, it was morning. He was the first up, feeling hung over and headache-y. Then he heard it—car traffic! He stumbled out onto the deck. They were back in a marina. Traffic was going by on the parkway.

Then he saw that the boat was actually tied up at the dock. Somebody had brought them in—through all that fog—and tied up the boat.

He awakened Alan and Peter. They were as surprised as he was. The three of them tried to find someone who had seen the boat coming in, but no one could tell them anything.

The strangest part was that they weren't at Mike's dock. They were in Sheepshead Bay, where Mike had seen the boat for the first time. Only one person could have brought them there, and that person had been lost at sea.

Specter at the Helm

Captain Joshua Slocum was a nautical dreamer whose home became the oceans of the world. Slocum was born in Nova Scotia in 1844. While working as an apprentice boot maker, he yearned to sail aboard the tall ships he had admired from his window. Dreams became reality when he abandoned the boot shop and became a ship's cook.

As the years passed, Slocum worked his way up the ranks, sailing aboard large ships that took him to Africa, China, Australia, and the East Indies, as well as to exotic ports of call in the South Pacific.

Eventually he received his master's license and commanded many vessels while logging thousands of miles across the seven seas.

Captain Slocum earned a unique place in maritime history when he became the first to sail a

small boat alone around the world. His experience as a master navigator served him well for this journey, but he was not prepared for the eerie encounter he had with an unusual sailor during a three-year voyage aboard the *Spray*.

It happened while Slocum was sailing alone near the Azores. He became ill and was soon huddled in pain on the deck of his tiny cabin. A violent storm erupted, but he was too weak to go topside and trim the sails.

Hours later, the gale was still raging as Slocum sat up and looked out of the companionway. He felt uneasy and stared in confusion at the sight of a man at the helm, holding the *Spray* on a steady course.

The oddly dressed helmsman stared at Slocum and said: "I'm from Christopher Columbus's crew, and the pilot of the *Pinta*. I've come to guide your boat."

Slocum collapsed and slept through the night. When he awoke the next morning he felt better and the storm had abated. The mysterious helmsman was gone. Slocum could not decide if he had been dreaming, hallucinating, or had actually seen the ghostly image at the wheel.

The sails should have been ripped to shreds by the winds, yet they were intact and set. Slocum calculated that the 36-foot yawl had traveled 90 miles, *on course,* throughout the stormy night. Only a skilled helmsman could have accomplished that incredible feat— perhaps one from the fifteenth century.

Haskell's Curse

One day in 1869 a workman was inspecting a fishing schooner, the *Charles Haskell,* for possible damage. He slipped on the steps of the companionway leading to the hold, fell, and broke his neck, dying instantly. A single mishap like this usually is chalked up to carelessness or coincidence. But this happened in Newfoundland, Canada, where fishermen who face the dangers of northern waters are likely to take every accident aboard ship as a sign that it is jinxed or cursed.

Certainly, the captain and crew of the *Haskell* believed this. They deserted the ship immediately. The owner, unable to find anyone willing to sign on, sold the schooner to a Captain Curtis of Gloucester, Massachusetts. The captain was a no-nonsense man who didn't believe in curses. He had some difficulty finding men to work for him at first, but the pay he offered was good, and soon he had a crew. The *Charles Haskell* was back fishing again on the Grand Banks, a series of shoals off Newfoundland.

Everything went well until 1870, when a hurricane struck the Grand Banks. The hundred or so fishing ships gathered there were tossed about like matchsticks. One huge comber lifted the *Charles Haskell* and hurled it like a battering ram against the *Andrew Johnson*, which was smashed to pieces, killing everyone aboard. Though badly crippled, the *Haskell* managed to limp back to port.

Most fishermen would have considered that part of the *Haskell*'s curse. But since it was the *Andrew Johnson* that went down, the crew felt it didn't apply to them. Once the ship was repaired, it was back on the Grand Banks again.

For six days the crew of the *Charles Haskell* fished without incident. But on midnight of the seventh day, the watchmen standing guard spied movement in the waters around the ship. As they watched, 26 figures wearing rain slickers began rising out of the sea. One by one, they boarded the schooner. Staring straight ahead through eyeless sockets, they took up stations along the ship's railing. There they went through the motions of fishing.

Frozen with terror, the guards were unable to move until the phantoms put away their imaginary nets and fishing rods and returned back to the sea. Then they rushed to the captain's cabin, babbling out an account of what they had seen.

Captain Curtis couldn't understand a word they were saying. But he saw stark fear in their eyes and ordered the ship back to port at once. It was well on its way by dawn. In the bright light of day the night's terrors seemed foolish. The captain was on the verge of returning to the Grand Banks when one of the crew shouted, "Look!"

Gaping, captain and crew watched at the 26 figures in rain slickers again rose from the sea and boarded the schooner. Once more they took up fishing positions along the rail. Finding his voice at last, the captain ordered full sail for port. But fast as the ship went, it could not shake the phantom fisherman. They stayed aboard until the port finally came into view. Then they climbed over the side of the ship. But this time, instead of sinking into the sea, they started walking across the sparkling waters towards the port, where they disappeared.

Who were they? Demons from the deep? The drowned men of the *Andrew Johnson*? No one took the time to ask. As soon as they docked, captain and crew fled, never to return.

No others came to take their place. The *Charles Haskell* was left to rot away in its berth. It never sailed again.

Saved by a Ghost

Some ghosts may not be much fun, but they are something better—protective spirits who warn the living of danger. They sometimes even actively save lives. Here are a few intriguing tales of their extraordinary helpfulness.

Night Train

The night train from London to Birmingham had stopped in the middle of a field. That wasn't unusual. In 1942, with bombings almost every night, you got used to messed-up schedules and unexpected delays. At least, ten-year-old Paul Kuttner was used to it. He was traveling alone, as he often did since his parents had been killed in the war, to visit a friend from boarding school during his summer vacation.

But there didn't seem to be any reason for the train to stop. There were no sounds of planes or sirens.

Paul saw, by the faint blackout glow of the lights on the side of the railroad car, that a couple of trainmen were standing alongside the tracks, looking up ahead.

He walked to one of the train doors, where some

passengers had already stepped out on the dark field. They were talking about something on the tracks, about 50 or 60 feet ahead. It looked like a man in a black cape with his arms stretched out to the sides above his head.

Paul jumped down from the train to look for himself. They were right. The man looked like Dracula. His arms—were they arms or wings?—in his cape were waving slowly and softly, almost rhythmically. Even with the train's headlights shining on the man, Paul couldn't see his face—or any of his features—just a blackness.

The engineer had been blowing the train's whistle trying to get the fellow to move, but there was no change in his position or his movements.

It was a warm summer night, but Paul started shivering.

More people were climbing out of the train now. A few of them yelled at the man—or the thing—on the tracks. A soldier gave two warning shots in the air with his rifle. But still the figure gave no indication that he heard them or that he would move.

At last, several of the braver passengers began walking up the tracks toward the dark figure. Paul started to go with them, but one of the trainmen pulled him back.

"You'd better stay here, lad," he said, putting a large, firm hand on Paul's shoulder.

As the group approached the figure, some of the passengers screamed. Paul could see them putting their arms out through the darkness. There was nothing there, they were saying. Nothing that they could feel, anyway!

A couple of the passengers walked farther down along the tracks, past where the figure seemed to be. Paul could see them talking and pointing and he could hear their voices getting higher, more excited, but he couldn't hear what they were saying.

The group of passengers was now half walking and half running back to the train, all talking at once.

Just beyond the spot where the shadow was, an overpass had been destroyed. If the train had gone just a few hundred feet farther, it would have smashed into the pile of rubble and derailed. Many of the passengers and crew surely would have been killed.

Suddenly a passenger pointed to the headlight.

"My God! Look at that," the man exclaimed.

And there, pressed against the train's headlight, was a butterfly. Either that, Paul thought, or a great moth. Its wings were spread and moving delicately.

"It's a butterfly that's casting a shadow," the train-man said loudly, very relieved, "just a butterfly!"

The butterfly, blocking some of the light, was casting a blacker shadow on the pile of rubble up ahead-a shadow that looked like a vampire. The waving of the figure's arms were the wing movements of the insect.

Why was no word given to the train company of the wrecked overpass? They found out later that the bombing had just taken place earlier that same night, and no one knew about it yet. Had the train not stopped, they all would have been killed. And nothing could have stopped the train, except perhaps a "butterfly."

Paul thought a lot about that in the days and years that followed. About what a lucky thing it was that a butterfly had settled on the headlight. And that it didn't just get smashed and die. And that the driver of the trains saw that there was something up ahead. And that he stopped in time. And that a few passengers walked ahead and found out about the overpass.

Was all that really luck? Or was it something else?

Protection from Beyond

In America's Old West, tomahawks were often the instrument of death for many courageous pioneers. At least once, however, this weapon played an exciting and mysterious part in saving a child from a tragic end.

A hardy settler and his family lived in a cabin far out in the wilderness. Wolves frequently raided the flocks, and were even said to attack people when hunger made them ravenous. To add to the dangers, Indians still roamed the area, looking for whatever they could steal. Occasionally they attacked a cabin, burned it, and killed its inhabitants.

One day the seven-year-old daughter of the family came upon a very old and sick Indian in the woods. Instead of running away in panic, she helped the ancient man to the cabin and pleaded with her folks to care for him. In spite of their misgivings, her par-

ents agreed. It soon became clear that he did not have long to live.

Although the old man could speak no English, he and the little girl became fast friends. She did everything she could to make his last days more comfortable, and he was obviously very grateful. Just before he died he called the girl and her parents to his bedside. Giving his tomahawk to the child, he motioned to the father to hang it on the wall over her small bed. His wish was granted, although the family could not understand why he insisted on it.

Some weeks later, while the father and mother were

away and the little girl was napping in her bunk, a gaunt wolf slipped out of the forest and headed for the cabin. He slunk up to the door, sniffed a few times, and then pushed against it. It swung open. He entered the house, his yellow eyes focusing on the tiny girl asleep in the bunk before him.

When the parents returned they were horrified to see a huge wolf apparently crawling into their cabin. They raced across the clearing, shouting, but the wolf did not move. He was dead, his skull crushed from a terrible blow on the head. Their daughter was still asleep in her bunk.

Later, the father jokingly said that perhaps the old Indian had come back to protect the little girl with his tomahawk. Something impelled him to lift the crude weapon from its peg over the bunk. As he looked at it, his laughter ceased.

The blade was splotched with dried blood and in the rawhide thong that bound the primitive blade to the stout handle were several long gray hairs, such as might be found on the head of a timber wolf!

Don't Jump Again

When Pauline Kane stepped aboard an airplane to go skydiving one afternoon, she could not know that her life would soon be changed by advice from a phantom.

The 26-year-old English girl sat patiently as the

plane gained altitude. When the signal was given by the pilot, she got in line with the other jumpers.

As she stood in the open doorway, she suddenly saw the image of her dead father. The apparition looked into her eyes and said: "Do not jump again after this."

Pauline was startled as she left the plane and floated safely down to the ground. She gathered her parachute and walked across the grassy field.

She was scheduled to go up later that afternoon, but decided to accept the eerie advice. She told the jumpmaster she had changed her mind about going up, but Pauline watched as the plane taxied out, rolled along the runway, and climbed steeply into the sky.

Moments later, the plane rolled over on its back and slammed into the ground. All six people aboard died instantly.

Spirits with a Message

G hosts return to earth for many different reasons. Some wish to help their loved ones, while others feel compelled to reveal the secrets of their death. Whatever the reason, the ghosts in this chapter feel the need to express themselves to the living.

Messages from the Dead

Many people know that Harry Houdini was obsessed, for the latter part of his life, anyway, with finding out if consciousness continued after death. He spent great amounts of time and money testing the mediums he had heard about to see if any were authentic. (Very few didn't resort to trickery at least some of the time.)

And he made a pact with his mother: After she died, she would send him a message that they set up in advance, a message only she, Houdini, and his wife, Bess, knew. That is, she would do it if it could be done.

He made a similar pact with Bess as well. Whoever died first would send back a message for the other. They devised a different secret message from the one

he had set up with his mother, and they told it to no one, so that, were the messages to get through, there could be no doubt that they were genuine.

Most people, though, aren't really sure what

happened after that. Did the messages get through or not? What were they?

This is what happened.

The psychic's name was Arthur Ford. He was not one of the mediums whom Houdini had discredited, but an ordained minister whose reputation was extraordinarily high. At a séance he was holding with a group of friends, Houdini's mother came through, saying that her message would open up the way for her son.

Her message started with FORGIVE and then went on to family matters. She instructed Arthur Ford to deliver the message to Bess, who confirmed that it was the one Houdini had waited in vain to hear ever since his mother died. Bess wrote that had he heard it in his lifetime, it probably would have changed the course of his life.

Then words from Houdini himself started to come to Ford—one or two at a time—as he did sittings with other people. Eventually the following message was pieced together:

A man who says he is Harry Houdini, but whose real name is Ehrich Weiss, is here and wishes to send to his wife, Beatrice Houdini, the ten-word code which he agreed to do if it was possible for him to communicate. He says you are to take this message to her and upon acceptance of it, he wishes her to follow out the plan they agreed upon before his passing. This is the code:

ROSABELLE ** ANSWER ** TELL ** PRAY ** ANSWER ** LOOK ** TELL ** ANSWER ** ANSWER ** TELL

The message went on, telling her to announce the receipt of his message, and not to be disturbed by what people would say. She was to return a code to him—which the two of them alone understood. And then, finally, he would give her the one word that he wanted to send back.

The next day, two members of the group who had been present at the sitting—one of them the associate editor of the *Scientific American*—went to see Bess and deliver the message from her husband.

"It is right!" she said, filled with emotion.

She invited Ford to come to her house the next day. After he went into a trance, the meeting went like this:

Ford: He tells you to take off your wedding ring and tell them what Rosabelle means.

Bess (*taking off her ring and singing*):

Rosabelle, sweet Rosabelle,

I love you more that I can tell;

O'er me you cast a spell,

I love you, my Rosabelle!

Ford: He says "I thank you, darling. The first time I heard you sing that song was in our first show together years ago."

Houdini went to give a much longer message—a very excited and enthusiastic one—about survival after death and how he wanted to let everyone know about it. If you want to read the other things he said, the book that tells it all is Arthur Ford's biography, *Nothing So Strange*.

After that, the code was explained:

ANSWER	B
TELL	E
PRAY, ANSWER	L
LOOK	I
TELL	E
ANSWER, ANSWER	V
TELL	E

Houdini's message was:
ROSABELLE, BELIEVE.

The Sound of the Drip

This eerie encounter is said to have taken place around West Chazy in New York State.

Not long ago a local resident, deciding to go fishing in a nearby pond, dug himself some worms, cut himself a nice pole and, taking along his dog, clambered into an old flat-bottomed boat for a quiet afternoon.

The dog curled up in the bottom of the boat and fell asleep almost as soon as the man had baited his hook and tossed it over.

The fish weren't biting. The man rowed from one spot to another, trying first here and then there along the shore. It was almost as though all of the fish in the pond had been caught or were in hiding.

Finally the man decided to try his luck in the middle of the little lake, where the water was deepest.

The moment he anchored there, the dog, who had been sound asleep the whole time so far, woke with a start and began to whine and tremble.

The man spoke sharply to him, telling him to be quiet and lie down. The dog obeyed, but he kept whining softly and trembling violently.

Hardly had the man dropped his hook to the bottom when he felt a tug. He began to pull on the line, but it seemed to hold fast to the bottom.

At this point, the dog jumped to his feet and began to bark viciously, showing his teeth and peering over the side of the boat, rocking it sharply. While struggling with the line, the man gave the dog a blow with one of the oars, sending him into the other end of the boat, where he cringed, whimpering.

Once more the man heaved his stout fishing pole. Slowly his catch—whatever it was—came to the surface. Tangled on the end of the line was a great clump of what looked like human hair. Shining in it was a bright golden barrette.

As the object appeared at the side of the boat, the

dog let out a howl of terror and plunged into the lake, heading for shore. He soon made it to land and vanished into the woods.

The man was amazed at the actions of the dog, but nevertheless decided to take the hair home and give the barrette to his wife. She could use it, he thought, to hold her hair back.

The barrette was so entangled that they would need to hang the hair before the fire to dry out to make removal easier. His wife, though horrified at the idea, coveted the bright barrette and so consented.

Long after the strands of hair were dry, the sound of dripping could still be heard.

It went on all evening. Then, at the stroke of twelve, a woman's voice came from the hanging strands. It told of her murder and how her body could be recovered. Then the voice faded away and was heard no more.

The man and his wife couldn't believe what they'd heard and decided to keep it to themselves for the time being, particularly so that the wife could keep the valuable barrette.

However, the dripping sound continued. It went on all night and all the next day, and the day after that. Finally, they could stand it no longer and reported their find to the authorities. Police dredged the lake and recovered the body, which was identified by the golden barrette.

The dog never returned.

Against All Odds

On the afternoon of April 16, 1951, the HMS *Affray* slipped away from the dock and sailed for Portsmouth. The British submarine was on a routine training cruise and informed her base she was beginning her dive at 9:15 PM.

It was the last message she would send.

The communications staff at Portsmouth became worried when the *Affray* failed to make any additional reports.

On April 17, the Admiralty initiated search operations on a massive scale. All attempts to signal the sub by radio were answered with silence as the search armada crisscrossed thousands of square miles off the English and French coastlines.

When no trace was found of the submarine and

her 75 crewmen after 2 days, search operations were suspended.

The job of finding *Affray*'s watery grave fell to HMS *Reclaim*, a salvage vessel that would investigate a wide expanse of ocean, scattered with more than 200 sunken ships. Fortunately, time and manpower could be saved during the arduous task by using underwater television cameras attached to the hull of the salvage ship.

After scanning the sea bottom for two months, the weary crewmen of the *Reclaim* were ready to give up. The submarine could not be located among the sunken vessels within the search grid. Many sailors felt the chances of finding the elusive *Affray* were a million to one.

Meanwhile, the wife of a British admiral was getting ready for bed one night when she suddenly felt she was not alone. She turned and was startled to see a naval officer near the door. She recognized the man at once, for he had often been a guest in their home while serving with her husband during the war. He stood very still, his eyes staring vacantly, and she was confused by his sorrowful expression.

"Tell your husband we are at the north end of Hurd Deep, nearly 70 miles from the lighthouse at St. Catherine's Point," said the officer. "It happened very suddenly and none of us expected it."

Before she could speak, the man disappeared.

After recovering her composure she called her husband, who was then logging time at a desk. She told him of the mysterious visit from their friend.

After the admiral passed the officer's mystical message to the Admiralty, the HMS *Reclaim* quickly weighed anchor and sailed to the new search area.

On June 14, as television cameras under the salvage ship were scanning a wreck on the outskirts of Hurd Deep, the operator spotted a nameplate belonging to the missing submarine. Her hull lay peacefully on the seabed where she came to rest 40 miles from her diving point. The doomed submarine was never raised, so the cause of her distress was never determined.

One fact was certain: HMS *Affray*'s last resting place would still be unknown if the admiral's wife had not been told its true position by one of the sub's officers, who came to visit their home one last time.

The Most Honored Ghost

The most famous phantom in all Australia is the ghost of Frederick George James Fisher of Campbelltown, New South Wales, who was murdered in 1826. Fisher was a convict sent to Australia for a minor offense. He made good in his new country as the first man to manufacture paper in New South Wales and he accumulated enough capital to purchase a 30-acre farm watered by a stream that flowed through his property.

The land next to Fisher's was rented by George Worrall, another convict settler. The two men became close friends. For a time Fisher even lived at Worrall's home.

Then, on June 17, 1826, Fisher suddenly disappeared. Worrall explained that his friend had run away to England to escape a charge of forgery that was being brought against him. Meanwhile, Worrall claimed that, in his absence, Fisher had made him overseer of his estate.

As time went on, Worrall began taking more and more liberties with Fisher's possessions. People began whispering about murder, especially when Worrall tried selling a horse that had belonged to Fisher. The whispers grew louder when he tried to sell Fisher's property. Finally, Worrall offered to pay $80 for the title deed to Fisher's land, which was being held against a debt Fisher owed a man named Daniel Cooper.

But suspicions are only suspicions, and there was still no real proof that Fisher had not fled to England as Worrall claimed.

Then one day a special constable named Farley was walking along the fence that separated Fisher's farm from Worrall's. He was startled to see a man either climbing or leaning against the fence in the southeastern corner of the Fisher property. The man's face was turned toward the creek, but Farley recognized the figure as Fisher. As Farley watched, Fisher raised his arm, pointing his forefinger in the direction of the creek.

Astonished at the man's sudden return, Farley called out Fisher's name. At this, the figure vanished. Farley hurried to the section of the fence where he had seen the ghost. Examining the rails, he saw massive blood stains.

With this new information, a concentrated search was made for Fisher's corpse. On October 20, 1826, two state troopers uncovered it in a swampy section the creek bank, exactly where the ghost had pointed. Worrall was taken into custody, tried, convicted, and hanged in February 1827.

As for Farley, any suspicion that he might have made up the story to urge on the investigation was dispelled as he lay dying in 1841. When asked by reporters if he had concocted the story, he replied, "I'm a dying man. I'll speak only the truth. I saw that ghost as plainly as I see you now."

Fisher's body was buried in the graveyard of St.

Peter's Church in Campbelltown. The grave was unmarked, and today its exact location is unknown. But Fisher's ghost is not forgotten. A festival to celebrate its appearance was first held in Campbelltown in 1856. Since then, the week-long festival in honor of the ghost has been held every year or two. A Fisher's Ghost Ball and other entertainments do honor to the age-old phantom. He is probably the only ghost in the world who is honored with a festival.

N ot all ghosts are frightening. Some of them seem to
be enjoying themselves, at least for a while. Others
are occasionally downright good company. You'll meet a
variety of social spirits in these odd tales.

Sam Plays the Ghost from Troy

A ghost in South Troy, New York, was a kindly soul who paid dividends in dollars for decent behavior toward him. His story has been circulating for many years now, and it goes like this.

Although the old house in South Troy was quite well furnished, it was never occupied for long. The tenants always found some excuse for moving out after a few weeks or even days. They said it was too scary to live in, and all gave the same account as to why.

It seems that every midnight a white-bearded old man, tall and thin, came clumping down from the attic and stalked into the parlor, where he stopped in front of some oil paintings and tapped them with his cane or pointed at them. After this he would clump out again and up to his attic. No one could touch him or stop him, but everyone could see him. It was said that if you stood in front of him he would walk right through you and it felt like a cool breeze blowing in your face. He'd never stop, even if the doors were locked shut before him.

Many tenants, as might be expected, told their stories to Sam, the saloonkeeper at Jefferson and First Streets. Sam never blinked. The owner of the house was beginning to think he would never rent the place to anyone, when he hit on an idea. He offered Sam and two friends of his a hundred dollars each to spend the night there. The landlord figured the saloon keeper would see no ghost and would soon dispel the fear in South Troy. Sam agreed and took his friends to the house to play pinochle.

But at the stroke of midnight, the old man did clump down again, and Sam saw him, just as he had been described. Without a word he went to the oil paintings, tapped each with his cane, then started back up toward the attic. Sam stood in his way and got walked through, but it didn't perturb him. It seemed to Sam that the old man was rather lonely and unhappy if he went about walking through people without saying hello.

Sam ran around to the front of the old man and gestured toward the pinochle table, offering him a chance to sit in on a few hands. The old man frowned, for a few moments puzzled. Then he floated over to the table and sat down. He couldn't hold the cards too well, due possibly to fluctuations in his ectoplasm. Occasionally his fingers would become transparent and the cards would fall to the table. He would seem to apologize. Also, Sam reported,

he played a rather naïve game of pinochle. Sam debated whether to throw the game to make the old man happy, but he decided against it.

After a half hour of pinochle the old man was apparently bored. He rose, banged heavily on the oil paintings with his cane—one, two, ten times—and clumped back up to the attic, nodding politely to Sam, but yawning nevertheless.

After some thought, Sam went to the paintings and took them down. The wallpaper behind them had a fist-size hollow with no plaster behind it. Sam stuck his hand through the paper and pulled out more than $50,000 in United States Government War Bonds. He later used them to open a large cocktail lounge on Second and Washington Streets.

The old man continued to be seen, however. It is said he clumps down from the attic even today. All his hoard is gone and he carries no cane or pointer, merely a mournful expression on his face, as if he feels he may have paid too much for a half hour's entertainment!

Lucky at Cards

It was a cold and stormy night in the late 1890s. The patrons of the Buxton Inn in Maine were sitting around a roaring fire in the taproom, swapping yarns. Suddenly, a young man entered. His rich clothes were trimmed with gold lace and he carried a cape over his arm. He shook the snow from his tall beaver hat, stamped his booted feet, and strode to the fireplace.

The others looked up with interest, admiring his elegance, but also noting that his clothes were old-fashioned and a bit strange. Undoubtedly, they thought, he was a traveler from some distant city. One of them offered him a place close to the fire, and suggested that he join them in a game of cards. With a cheerful smile he agreed.

As the evening and the game progressed, the young man had uncanny good luck in every deal of the cards. The other players all felt that there was something familiar about the handsome young man, as though they had seen him many times before but couldn't place him. Oddly enough, he knew many of them by name, but never introduced himself.

It was nearly morning when another patron entered. As he removed his coat and boots, he called to the innkeeper. "What's happened to your sign? I thought I had the wrong tavern."

The others, surprised, looked out the window to see the swinging sign outside the door. Wiping the steam from the glass, they saw with astonishment that there was nothing upon the sign but the words BUXTON INN. The painting of a young cavalier was gone. Then they knew.

With wonder and fright they turned back to the fireplace, but the dapper young card player was gone, leaving nothing but a small puddle of melted snow beneath the chair where his boots had rested. No wonder he had looked familiar.

Almost fearfully they turned again to look at the tavern's sign. Was it a trick of the storm? For now, as clearly as ever, they could see the painting of young Charles in his tall beaver hat and flowing cape, as he had stood for many years. Then something else caught their eye—something they had never noticed before. One of the pockets of his breeches seemed to be bulging as though with many coins, and a smile played about the painted mouth—the kind of smile a young man might wear when he has been lucky at cards.

A Night with the Dead

It happened in the 1890s. A husband and wife driving a buggy along a New England road were overtaken by darkness. Not knowing how far it would be to the next town, they started looking for a place to spend the night. Soon they spotted a light to one side of the road and up a lane through the trees. They turned their tired horse and drove toward it.

The light turned out to be in a small farmhouse on a little hill between two huge elms. The husband rapped on the door, while his wife sat in the buggy.

An aged couple came to the door with a kerosene lamp. When the situation was explained to them, they invited the travelers in for the night. The two couples got along pleasantly, found that they had much in common and, after a warming cup of tea, they all retired. The host refused any payment for the lodgings.

The next morning the travelers rose early to be on their way. So as not to embarrass their host and hostess, they left some silver coins on the table in the hall before they slipped out of the house to hitch up their horse.

Driving to the next town, which proved to be just a couple of miles farther through the woods, they stopped at an inn for breakfast.

Over coffee, they mentioned to the innkeeper where they had stayed the night before and how much they had enjoyed talking with the old couple. The innkeeper looked at them in astonishment. They couldn't have done any such thing, he told them, for he knew the house and the Edmundses, who had lived there. The Edmundses had died twenty years before.

The travelers were incredulous. Edmunds was the name the old couple had given them. Their descriptions of the couple tallied with the innkeeper's but the travelers *knew* they had spoken with the Edmundses and had tea with them.

"Impossible," scoffed the innkeeper. The Edmundses burned to death in a fire that had completely destroyed their home, and it had never been rebuilt. The argument mounted. Finally the travelers insisted on driving the innkeeper back to the farm to prove they had slept there the night before.

Back they went the two miles. There, to their horror, all they found was an empty cellar hole overgrown with weeds and filled with burned timbers and blackened furniture. The couple could not believe their eyes. Then it was the innkeeper's turn to pale, because with a cry of terror, the wife pointed a shaky finger at a spot in the charred rubble below them.

On what might have been a hall table shone a half dollar and two quarters, just the amount the travelers had left in payment that morning while the Edmundses were still "asleep."

Return from the Dead

Why do some ghosts return from the dead? Do they need one last fling, or is it just too hard for them to accept their death? Here are a few stories about ghosts who made one last appearance before leaving earth for good.

Valentine's Visit

It was Valentine's Day and 18-year-old Teresa was in despair. On February 12th she received an eviction notice from the tiny apartment she shared with her mother, who had died two weeks before. And she found herself unable to do anything about it.

She couldn't get herself to go into her mother's room, much less go through her things. She couldn't find a mover on such short notice who would move her from Baltimore to her uncle's house in Washington, D.C., 38 miles away, and her uncle was an old man who could not be of much help. Teresa had always been a sickly, solitary person and she had no friends she could call upon.

If only Jimmy were here, she thought, he could take care of everything. Jimmy was her brother who was

serving in Vietnam, and he hadn't been heard from for a long time. The Red Cross had tried to bring him home for the funeral, but it seemed that they were unsuccessful. They did report, however, that he had been notified of his mother's death.

Suddenly, as Teresa sat on the couch with her hands over her face, Jimmy was in the room, handsome as always and in uniform. The Red Cross must have succeeded after all!

What happened then seemed like a dream.

Jimmy went into their mother's bedroom with Teresa and helped her pack the things. Then he brought her back into the living room and told her to call a mover.

"I tried," Teresa told him, "and no one would do it."

"Try again," Jimmy said.

This time Teresa found a mover who had just had a cancellation and could do the moving that very day.

While they waited for the movers to come, Teresa and Jimmy packed up the few possessions in the apartment without saying a word.

Then, when the movers arrived, Jimmy took Teresa by the shoulders and said, "You go with the truck, and don't look back. Do what Mother always wanted you to do, and remember, I'll always be with you."

When Teresa boarded the moving truck, the men

asked her why her brother wasn't coming along to Washington.

"I guess he had to get back," she said, wondering about that herself.

It wasn't until March, 10, 1964, that Teresa found out why Jimmy didn't come along to Washington. She received a telegram, forwarded from her old address, telling her that her brother had been killed in Vietnam on February 14th—the very same day he was with her.

Stopover in a Small Town

On the afternoon of February 1, 1963, Thomas P. Meehan completed arbitrating a case for the State Department of Employment Appeals Bureau in Eureka, California. At two o'clock the 38-year-old attorney began the drive to his home in Concord.

He never made it.

While cruising along Highway 101, he began to feel drowsy and stopped at Myers Flat. He called his wife and said he was not feeling well. She suggested he get a good night's rest at a motel and come home the following morning.

Meehan drove to Redway and took a room at the Forty Winks Motel. At 5:00 PM he tried to call his wife to let her know where she could reach him, but the phones were out of order.

One hour later he was feeling worse. He drove to Garberville and checked in at the emergency room of the Southern Humboldt Community Hospital. At 6:45 he told the duty nurse that he felt as if he were dead. She went to summon a doctor, but Meehan was not in the waiting room when they returned.

At seven o'clock, while driving on Highway 101

211

along the Eel River, a couple from Myers Flat told a Highway Patrol officer they had just seen a car veer off the road and crash into the river.

An hour later Meehan was back at the Forty Winks Motel, talking to owner Chip Nunnemaker. At nine o'clock, as the attorney said good night and headed for his room, Nunnemaker noticed fresh mud on Meehan's shoes and on the cuffs of his trousers. At the door, Meehan turned around and said, "Do I look like I'm dead? I feel like I've died and the whole world died with me."

Harry Young, a motel employee, went to Meehan's room 30 minutes later to tell him the phones were still not working, due to a storm. Meehan had changed clothes and was now wearing a black suit.

At 10:45 the Highway Patrol located Meehan's car in the Eel River, its taillights glowing faintly below the murky water.

The body of Thomas Meehan could not be found, but footprints were found leading up to the embankment for about 30 feet. Beyond that point the footprints ended and the mushy terrain was undisturbed.

On February 20, Thomas Meehan's body was recovered from the Eel River, about 16 miles from where his car went into the water. The coroner said Meehan had survived the crash, only to drown later.

Did the ghost of Thomas Meehan return to the Forty Winks Motel and talk with the owner an hour after crashing into the Eel River? It was during this time that Chip Nunnemaker saw mud on Meehan's shoes and pants. Did Harry Young see Meehan's apparition wearing a different suit at 9:30? Both men accepted Meehan as a living person.

Thomas Meehan never checked out of the motel, and no one saw him again until 19 days later when his body was found floating in the Eel River.

Had Meehan climbed 30 feet up the wet embankment? If so, what happened to him at the point where his footprints ended? Is that where he died and his spirit began wandering back and forth between the real world and eternity?

In the Midnight Hour

In April 1945, Allied forces in Europe were on the threshold of victory. Germany's generals had lost hope the previous summer, when Eisenhower's troops captured the beaches at Normandy.

Adolf Hitler committed suicide on April 30, and the war ended eight days later.

A few weeks earlier, an American infantry unit had taken Amsdorf, a sheep village on the west bank of the Elbe River. Lieutenant Al van Detta set up headquarters in one of the buildings and awaited further orders.

One morning Privates Jay F. Rivera and Richard O'Leary found their names on the list for sentry duty. At midnight they reported to their post and began their lonely task. Although only 19 years old, the 2 combat veterans were used to a lot more action than guarding a grove of trees at the edge of town.

Thirty minutes later, O'Leary could no longer tolerate the boredom. "I'm going to go get some coffee, Jay. I'll be right back."

It was a serious offense to leave your post, but Rivera knew he could handle the job alone. He settled down again and stared across the moonless terrain, wondering if any of the Führer's master race were lurking in the shrubbery.

215

About ten minutes later, Rivera heard someone approaching from behind. He turned around, expecting to see O'Leary, and was surprised to see Private Michael Prettyboy, a friend from another platoon.

"Hello, Michael," said Rivera. "What are you doing out here?"

"I couldn't sleep and decided to take a walk," answered Prettyboy. "How come you're alone on guard duty?"

"Oh, I'm not," said Rivera. "O'Leary's with me but he went to get some coffee. He'll be back soon."

The two friends talked about the war and told each other of their experiences during the past week.

Prettyboy then got up and grabbed his rifle. "I'll see you later, Jay. I've got guard duty myself in another hour."

O'Leary soon returned and the two boys remained at the isolated outpost until relieved at two o'clock.

Six hours later, Rivera was eating breakfast and overheard others talking about gunfire during the night. Apparently a sentry had fired at someone in the open field.

"You know," said Rivera. "It could have been Michael Prettyboy out there last night. He came across the field to see me when I was on guard duty."

Lieutenant van Detta stopped sipping coffee and looked suspiciously at Rivera. "Are you sure about that?"

"Yes, sir," said Rivera. "You can ask O'Leary."

"That won't be necessary," said van Detta.

Suddenly, Rivera felt uneasy and wondered if the platoon leader knew about O'Leary leaving his post the night before. Perhaps the lieutenant was trying to get him to confirm O'Leary's absence.

"Sir," pleaded Rivera, "I'm sure O'Leary will remember. Just ask him."

"I don't have to," said van Detta. "If you and O'Leary saw Prettyboy last night, you were either dreaming or drunk on duty. Private Prettyboy was killed in action yesterday morning."

A Patch of Fog

In the winter of 1918, Lieutenant David McConnel and Lieutenant Larkin were two young pilots in the Royal Flying Corps. On December 7, David McConnel was scheduled to deliver a Sopwith Camel to Tadcaster, only 60 miles away. He would be followed by another pilot who would pick him up and return to their base.

Larkin was reading a newspaper when he heard his roommate at the window.

"Hello," said Larkin. "I thought you were flying this morning."

"I'm on my way now," McConnel said with a grin. "But I forgot my map."

Larkin grabbed the chart from the desk and handed it to his friend.

"Thanks," said McConnel. "Should be back by

teatime," he added as he ran toward the flight line.

McConnel greeted the pilot who would bring him home in the two-seat Avro. They climbed into their planes, the engines came to life, and the two men were soon airborne.

En route they were forced to land because of

heavy fog. McConnel went to a phone and called his base. The commander advised him to return now if he thought it was unsafe to continue. McConnel felt confident he could complete the flight.

They took off, but the swirling fog only got worse. Halfway to Tadcaster, McConnel saw the Avro pilot descend and make an emergency landing in a field. McConnel continued, certain that he could find a hole and land at his destination.

At 3:25 that afternoon, Larkin was reading a book when McConnel came into the room. He was still wearing his flight suit and seemed happy to be home.

"Hello, David," said Larkin. "How was the flight?"

"Ran into some fog, but got there all right," said McConnel. "Had a good trip." As he turned to go, he said, "Cheerio," and then walked out.

Later, another friend dropped in to tell Larkin that he and McConnel planned to dine at the Albion Hotel in Lincoln. Larkin said he would join them.

When Larkin arrived at the hotel, he got a drink and looked for McConnel. He walked across the room and joined a crowd of fellow officers near the fireplace. At a nearby table, he overheard a pilot discussing an accident involving a Sopwith Camel.

When Larkin heard the word *Tadcaster,* he went to the table.

"Excuse me," he said, "but I thought I heard you mention Tadcaster. My roommate, Dave McConnel, took a Camel there this morning."

"Yes," said the pilot. "It's really a shame. Poor chap. We just got word at the base."

"What do you mean?" Larkin asked curiously. "I saw him this afternoon. He was in a cheerful mood."

"I'm really sorry," said the pilot. His expression seemed apprehensive as he glanced around the table, then looked at Larkin. "I don't think you saw your friend this afternoon. McConnel crashed while trying to land in heavy fog. He was killed instantly."

Larkin learned details of the accident the next day from the operations officer. When McConnel's plane nose-dived into the runway at Tadcaster his head smashed into the machine gun mount over the small windscreen.

David McConnel's wristwatch had stopped upon impact with the ground at 3:25—the precise time Larkin had seen him enter their room.

And Then There Were None

The Battle of Britain had just ended, and the Royal Air Force had won a momentary victory in the skies over London in the fall of 1940. The myth of the Luftwaffe's supremacy had been shattered as Germany's elite fighter squadrons retreated to consider their losses.

Although Britain's aerial triumph was only temporary, it gave Bomber Command time to attack German military installations along the occupied eastern coasts of the English Channel. These targets were heavily defended, but there was a chance to destroy them before the Luftwaffe had a chance to regroup.

One RAF squadron was selected to attack the critical German targets with tactics that were bold and extremely dangerous. The bombers would go in low, drop their bombs, and get away as fast as

their twin-engine planes could fly. The mission was so important that Bomber Command sent an air marshal to oversee the mission. He would debrief the aircrews upon their return and forward the information to headquarters.

Twelve A-20 Havoc medium bombers started their engines, taxied to the runway, and were soon airborne. The planes were American built and each carried a pilot, copilot, bombardier, and a 2,000-pound bombload.

Now came the worst part of the mission for those left behind—the waiting. As the sun began to slide below the horizon, the air marshal drank tea and calculated the time when he could expect the planes to return.

Hours later, he heard the distant drone of aircraft engines and went outside. He looked up at the sky as he walked to the Operations building, but it was too dark to see the approaching planes.

The marshal wondered how many crews had returned as the planes taxied to the parking area and shut down their engines. A few minutes later, he heard the sound of vehicles stopping outside; then nine weary airmen came into the room. Their haggard expressions revealed the terrible ordeal they had survived.

"At ease, men," said the air marshal. "I know you've seen a lot of sky today and I won't keep you longer than necessary." He paused, then realized he was looking at only three crews. Where were the men from the remaining nine bombers? "Did any more planes make it back?"

The weary airmen shook their heads, and one of the

pilots described the furious antiaircraft fire and flak that had covered the sky like a black blanket. He said the low-level bomb run had been successful, but very costly. The only planes to survive were those in the first wave. By the time the remaining bombers started their run, the German gunners had pinpointed the range and shot the planes to pieces.

Nine planes out of 12 had been lost, along with 27 men. It had been a catastrophe, and the air marshal found it difficult to believe that any planes had survived. The crewmen completed their written reports and signed their names.

"Well done, boys," said the air marshal. "You've earned a drink and a good night's rest. The bar is open."

The airmen departed and left the marshal to agonize over the fact that 75 percent of the attacking force had been destroyed during a single mission. Headquarters was not going to be satisfied with the disastrous news.

The air marshal's gloomy thoughts were interrupted by his aide, who walked to the table and sat down. "I don't quite know how to say this, sir, but we had some tremendous losses today."

"I know," the air marshal said and sighed. "We lost nine planes."

The aide looked puzzled. "No, sir, you've got the wrong number."

The air marshal's eyes reflected a flicker of hope.

"Did some of the planes land somewhere else? That's good news."

"Sir, I don't understand what you mean. We lost all of the planes on today's mission."

"You're mistaken," argued the marshal. "Three made it back here. I just debriefed the crews and sent them to the bar for a nightcap."

The aide stared at his superior in disbelief. "I don't know what you're talking about, sir. All of the bombers were shot down over the target."

The air marshal rose, took the written reports from his folder and tossed them on his table. "Then how do you explain these? I watched the men fill those out and sign them."

The aide stared at the documents and noticed that the names, ranks, and aircraft numbers were the same as three of the crews listed as killed in action that day.

"Are you telling me the men I debriefed are dead? Look at the dates and times."

"I'm sorry, sir," said the aide. "I can't explain it. But none of the planes landed here and the bar has been empty all night."

Confirmation came the next day. All 12 bombers had been shot down by German antiaircraft fire. There were no survivors. Another startling fact was discovered when the official results of the bombing attack arrived. The information contained in the reports made by the dead crewmen precisely matched the actual damage to the target.

Nine men had filled out the papers and signed their names. Nine men, who had died hours before they described the horrors of that tragic afternoon to the air marshal, had then walked out of the room and were never seen again.

Sometimes ghosts haunt people to get revenge. Some do it just for the fun of it. But a few have appeared for a very specific purpose—to warn someone of approaching death.

The White Bird of Death

Whenever a member of the Oxenham family dies, a white bird is seen, usually in the bedroom (or trying to enter the bedroom) of the dying person. Sometimes the bird is seen in other places as well. This has been going on for almost 400 years. A close family member generally sees the bird. Sometimes, doctors and nurses and ministers see it, or hear it. But it always makes an appearance.

One of the most famous instances was the death of Margaret Oxenham. She had been unable to decide which of two men she should marry. Finally she made up her mind, and on her wedding day a huge feast was held at the manor. The bride's father was having a grand time, until he saw a white bird fluttering around his daughter's head. No one else seemed to notice it or hear it, least of all Margaret.

The next day was the wedding. Margaret made the right decision which man to marry, but the wrong one for her safety, because the rejected suitor leaped out of the crowd, either stabbed or shot her (there are two stories), and then killed himself.

A more recent occurrence deals with the death of

Mrs. John Oxenham in 1975. Mrs. Oxenham's daughter, who lived in London, was making a trip to Cornwall to see her sick mother, but she had no idea that the illness was life-threatening. So she stopped off to visit a friend along the way. During her visit, a large white bird stayed around outside the house, perching on the windowsill and the roof. No one said very much about it at first, but after it was seen by many people for several days, they began to talk about it. No one had seen a bird like that in the area before.

"Oh, no, could that be *the* white bird?" Mrs. Oxenham's daughter wondered. She had never connected this white bird to the legend. Was *she* was going to die?

Frightened, she packed quickly and left for Cornwall. The bird left when she did. A week later, Mrs. John Oxenham was dead.

The Psychic Mice

Actor Raymond Massey and his wife, Dorothy, were tired of staying at hotels whenever they came to New York and they decided to find a small house where they could stay that they could eventually call home.

Dorothy did the house-hunting and came up with two brownstone townhouses that she liked. First she took Ray to see her favorite, but from the moment he walked into it, he disliked it intensely. It felt cold, he said, like a tomb.

The other house was right across the street. He agreed with Dorothy on that one, and they bought it.

One day after they had settled in, Dorothy was out walking the dog when she met a woman who turned out to be her new neighbor from across the street.

"I liked your house so much," Dorothy told her, "I thought it was much nicer than ours, but Ray didn't like it."

"It's a nice house," said her neighbor, "but we've got such a problem with mice. I've tried everything, but I can't get rid of them."

A short time after that, Dorothy was looking out the window, and couldn't believe what she saw. Waves of mice were coming out of the basement of the house across the street. They were disoriented, running, stumbling, scurrying along the street. Dorothy had heard of rats leaving a sinking ship, but she found it hard to believe that mice would choose to leave a perfectly good brownstone.

A few days later, Ray called her attention to a front-page story about a socialite who had committed suicide.

"That must be the woman who lives across the street," Dorothy said. "Check the address." It was the woman who owned the house with the mice—without the mice, now.

The next occupant turned out to be a beautiful blonde, who was dating a famous, wealthy playboy. Just before his death made front-page news, another generation of mice moved out of the house.

Dorothy began watching the house across the street with a kind of horror. It stayed vacant for quite a while. Finally, it was purchased by an "important" businessman, and she stopped paying attention.

One day when she was watering some plants in the window box, she saw the mice again—going through the same routine. What was going to happen now?

She didn't have to wait long to find out. It was on the front page of the *Times* again. A prominent businessman who flew his own plane was coming home from a trip to Canada, when his plane experienced technical problems and fell into the Hudson River. He drowned before rescuers could reach him.

They recognized the address—it was the house across the street!

Then a strange thing happened. The Masseys had had mice in the house themselves ever since the first exodus of mice across the street. Nothing seemed to get rid of them—even cats. But suddenly their own mice began to leave. Can you imagine what went on in their heads?

No, nothing terrible happened to Dorothy or Ray. But the mice were smart to leave, because shortly afterward, the furnace blew up.

Fatal Warnings

Men who spend much of their lives at sea are full of tales of premonitions and strange apparitions.

Take, for example, the strange dream of the women in white in the rain that plagued John Nelson, the cook aboard the schooner *Sachem*, out of Gloucester. The *Sachem*, under the command of Captain J. Wenzell, had been out fishing. On September 7, 1871, she pulled her hook and sailed away, to try for better luck.

That night, as recorded in the log and journal of Captain Wenzell, John Nelson hurried aft to talk to the captain. He was greatly agitated and apparently in mortal fear.

He told the captain that he had just awakened from a dream that he had had twice before in his

life—a dream that had been followed both times by shipwreck and tragedy. Nelson had dreamed of women, dressed all in white, standing in the rain as though waiting for their men to come back, perhaps from the sea. The cook then begged the captain to head for port or at least to get away from the dangerous Georges Bank, noted for storms and reefs.

The captain made little of Nelson's fears and urged him to go back to his galley and prepare the evening meal. Mumbling that it would be fatal to stay there after the warning of the "women all in white," Nelson left.

Later that night it began to blow. About 1:30, one of the men reported in alarm that the *Sachem* was taking in water. Captain Wenzell hurried below and found six inches of water already sloshing in the hold. He quickly ordered that the pumps be manned and a bucket brigade be formed to empty the ship, but, despite their efforts, they could not keep ahead of the inrushing water. The cook was ordered to provision a lifeboat and be ready to leave if necessary.

Believing that the leak might be on the other side, the captain tacked the schooner in the other direction in an attempt to bring the leak above the waterline. This didn't help. In desperation they signaled another schooner, the *Pescador*. At great risk the ships were brought together and the men of the doomed schooner were taken off. Shortly after, the *Sachem* rolled over on her side and then slid below the waves, bow first. Once more, the "women all in white" had been right!

I n and of themselves, inanimate objects cannot be evil,
carry curses, or warn of disasters and death. Can
they? But what if they do? The objects in this chapter certainly seem intent on bringing death and destruction to all
they encounter.

The Jinxed Ship

Heading a squadron of British men-of-war, the ship called the *Bacchante*, homeward bound from Australia to England, traveled through the Pacific on an early June day in 1881. Smoke poured from her high stacks; she was in a hurry to get home after an extensive tour of Far East duty.

Suddenly, amid a clamor of engine-room bells, the great ship's speed began to slacken. Officers on the bridge turned their binoculars westward, and men hurried to the starboard rail.

For, standing in stark relief near the horizon, was a sailing ship on fire.

Or was it on fire? Rather, the vessel was bathed in a strange red light. Two other warships in the squadron, the *Cleopatra* and the *Tourmaline*, flashed signals to the *Bacchante* asking about the "strange glow."

The sailing ship came to within 200 yards of the *Bacchante* and sailed serenely across her bows. As she turned, the name on her stern could be seen clearly. She was the *Libera Nos*, ghost ship of the Pacific.

A murmur of consternation ran through the *Bacchante*'s crew. Quickly, Captain George Francis rang for full speed, and instructed his men to get back to their duties. It was a time when every man needed his mind fully focused. They all knew what it meant for the *Libera Nos* to cross a vessel's bows: Disaster and tragedy would inevitably follow.

Legends had quickly woven themselves around the disappearance of the brig ten years earlier. It was said that her master, Captain Bernard Fokke, in order to make port in record time, had gambled with the Devil and lost.

Since that day, the "ship of death" with a crew of skeletons sailed the Pacific, sending ships to their doom.

Some sailors had claimed to have seen a skeleton captain standing on the fo'c'sle head holding a telescope and an hourglass.

The traditions of the Royal Navy made no concessions to mystery and sea lore. The day's entry in the log of the *Bacchante*, in its usual matter-of-fact phrasing, serves only to make more bizarre the facts it contains:

"There is no doubt that a ship bathed in a strange red glow did approach us. Our lookout man on the forecastle reported her as close to our starboard bow, where also the officer of the watch on the bridge clearly saw her.

"At least 100 persons saw her, yet soon after she had crossed our bows and her name had become visible, she appeared to vanish.

"There was no vestige nor any sign of any material ship to be seen either rear, or away to, the horizon. Whether it was the *Libera Nos* or one of the other alleged phantom ships which are claimed to haunt the area must remain unknown.

"During the forenoon watch, the seaman who had first reported the phantom vessel fell from our foremast crosstrees and was killed instantly. He was a smart seaman, one of the most promising hands the ship, and every man on board feels sad and despondent at his loss."

That was not the end. When the squadron reached port, the commander was stricken with a fatal illness, and the *Cleopatra* was badly damaged while docking.

The *Libera Nos* was seen again in 1893 by a clipper bound for New Zealand. Two years later, a homeward-bound Australian captain logged her as "painted bright yellow, three-masted, and what sails she wore hung tattered from square yards."

In 1899 the steamship *Hannah Regan*, bound for Europe with more than a million dollars' worth of gold, lost her propellers and was badly damaged in heavy weather. She sank in deep water near Okinawa. Her log, along with the bodies of the captain, first mate, and four of her crew, drifted ashore in an open boat some weeks later.

The log referred to a "phantom brig, bathed in a red-gold glow." Ominously, that was the last entry.

Salvage operations were planned. An oceangoing tug sailed from San Francisco and located the wreck. That evening, the captain of the tug was strolling around his deck when he noticed a shadow about half a mile out to sea.

"Slowly the shadow assumed the shape and appearance of a sailing vessel. She was heading in our direction and driving along as if in the grip of violent winds, although there was no wind and the sea was flat calm.

"She came right alongside and I doubted my own shocked senses, for I could see right through her, though every detail of her deck work and rigging stood out clearly. As I watched, she sank slowly beneath the sea and disappeared."

The salvage crew assembled shortly after dawn the next day and got to work. Two divers went down into the wreck—and never emerged. Both were found dead with their windpipes severed. There was no rational explanation for the tragedy.

The salvage attempt met with so many mishaps that it was eventually abandoned, leaving all that was left of the *Hannah Regan* and her cargo of gold to be torn apart by the sea.

But the ship of death sailed on. During World War II, German U-boat crews claimed to have seen the phantom while on tours of duty east of Suez. Some asked for a transfer to Atlantic duty rather than run the risk of seeing the ghost ship again.

And every one of the U-boats that encountered the *Libera Nos* was lost on subsequent missions.

The Turquoise Ring

The ring was made in 1913. It was 14-carat gold with a square turquoise stone held in place by two beautifully sculpted nymphs. It was bought by Captain Albrecht Halberstern of the Eleventh Saxon Artillery Regiment, who sent the ring to his wife in Dresden. He went on to survive three years of combat on the Western Front, earned the Iron Cross, and returned home in November 1918. His wife had been killed the day before, while wearing the ring. She was hit through the temple by a stray bullet when she went out on her balcony. She was the only person to be killed in Dresden that day.

The ring was sold to a jeweler named Pecht. Soon after buying it he went bankrupt and drowned himself.

Meanwhile, Captain Halberstern was feeling sen-

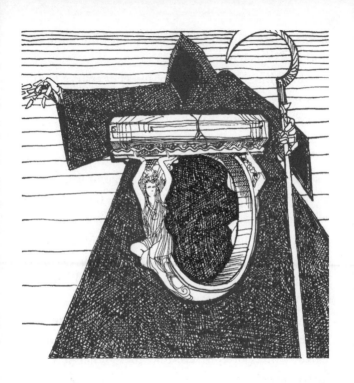

timental about his wife's jewelry. He bought back
the ring, planning to wear it himself. He was wearing it when he went out riding in June 1929; his

horse threw him and his injuries left him paralyzed and in a wheelchair.

After Hitler came to power, the Halberstern family was sent to Auschwitz. The captain never made it all the way. His body was thrown from a cattle car with the dead.

The turquoise ring was rescued, however. It found its way into the possession of a Nazi labor front functionary named Kurt Weichter. He gave the ring to his wife on their 20th wedding anniversary, and then his work took him to Czechoslovakia. He missed the infamous air attack on Dresden in which his wife, parents, two children, and their dog were killed.

The turquoise ring survived the firestorm. It was the only possession Weichter had when the war ended. He sold it to a U.S. Army sergeant for 12 cartons of cigarettes. He told the soldier it was a good luck charm.

The sergeant gave the ring to his fiancée, who gave it back when the engagement was broken off a month later. The sergeant's fingers were too thick to wear the ring, so he put it on a chain and wore it around his neck. He was wearing it on his wedding day when he and his new bride were driving out on a honeymoon trip to Lake Superior. His car collided with a truck at 70 miles per hour. Both the sergeant and his wife were killed instantly. The ring wasn't even dented. It went to his sister Caroline.

Caroline managed to wear the ring for six years without incident. Then her home was burgled by a young man named Robert Saugasso. He died not long afterwards, soon after falling—or being pushed—out a window. In his room, the police found the ring and returned it to Caroline.

Caroline was getting uncomfortable about the ring and tried to sell it. Not soon enough. Her marriage broke up and she was left with two young children and a husband who seldom paid child support. She finally sold the ring to an antique dealer named Landau.

The ring stayed in the Landau's window for a year. The shop burned down. The ring was fine.

Landau had a heart attack and died. His stock was auctioned off.

That's the last anyone knows of the turquoise ring. If you see it—a gold ring with nymphs and a big square stone—in a jeweler's window or at an auction or estate sale, beware.

The Killer Lake

Lake Fundudzi, in the African Transvaal, is said to be sacred to the spirit of the python that lives in it. No one bathes or fishes in the lake, though it is large and fed by many small rivers. Some say it is poisonous, because it has no fish or other marine life, but crocodiles thrive in it. Stranger still, no one has ever taken any specimens of the black, muddy water so that it can be scientifically analyzed.

Dr. Harry Burnside had heard about the lake. He knew that human sacrifices had once been made there, and perhaps some still were, secretly. And he had heard that there was a death curse on any white man who disturbed the peace of the lake.

He had heard the story about the Van Blerk brothers, too. They didn't believe in curses or

taboos. Jacobus van Blerk had watched his brother, Hendrik, put a six-foot collapsible canoe into the lake and paddle out on the still water. Suddenly the canoe stopped moving, although Hendrik was still paddling furiously. Then it abruptly disappeared under the water, as though a force reached up and pulled it down to the bottom. That was in 1947. Twenty-seven-year-old Hendrik van Blerk and his canoe were never seen again.

But Harry Burnside believed only in science. And for the sake of science, he determined to go to the lake in 1953 and bring back some water for examination. He took with him six bottles of several different types, with several different types of stoppers. At least one of them, he thought, would get through. He also brought along his assistant, 22-year-old William Thacker. They couldn't persuade any natives to go with them. So, they set out alone.

They parked their car seven miles from the lake and went the rest of the way on foot. They had no choice. Sometimes they had to cut through heavy brush to get to the lake.

They arrived after nightfall, so they camped close by. At dawn, they saw that the water had receded five feet from where it had been the night before. It was inky and still. But now the level was rising.

Burnside put his finger in the water and brought a drop to his mouth. Bitter, it stung his tongue.

The men filled their bottles and closed them, and then investigated the plants growing around the lake. They had never seen anything like some of them before, so they collected a few specimens to take back with them.

In the late afternoon, they started back to the car,

but by nightfall, they had only gotten halfway. They camped out, agreeing to take turns staying awake to guard against wild animals. During the night, Thacker heard a popping sound and woke Burnside, but they couldn't find any reason for it. They checked the bottles, which were fine.

At dawn, they checked the bottles again before packing up. *Every one of them was empty*. One, that had a slip-on top, had burst. The others were still closed but nothing was in them. The water could not possibly have leaked out.

They returned to the lake and refilled the bottles. Burnside was not feeling well.

They returned to the car in the afternoon and checked the bottles again. They were all right. They drove back to the local town from which they had started. When they arrived, they re-checked the bottles. They were still full.

Both Burnside and Thacker were disturbed about the Fundudzi trip, but managed to get some sleep that night. Then, in the morning, they checked the bottles again. Not a drop of the murky black water was left. None of the bottles had been opened.

Burnside now had severe stomach pains. Nine days later, he had to be taken to the hospital. As soon as he possibly could, Thacker took the plants to an expert to have them classified. The expert told him that the specimens were too old. Thacker couldn't believe it! In spite of all his efforts to keep them fresh, the plants had deteriorated to the point where they looked as if they were at least 50 years old.

Burnside went into a delirium that lasted ten hours. He died the next day. The doctors said it was enteritis, inflammation of the intestines. Could it have been from touching a drop of the inky black water to his tongue? Could it have been that poisonous? Or was something deadlier at work?

Seven months later, Thacker was out sailing when he was thrown into the water and drowned.

Coincidence? Some people said so. But the natives thought otherwise. Lake Fundudzi had taken another victim.

Wake of the Wicked Clipper

The *Squando* was a jinx even before she slid down the ways in Oslo, Norway. Half a dozen men were killed or injured while building the big clipper ship in 1884.

Before the ship was completed, the widow of a worker who had been killed came to the shipyard and shouted, "I curse this ship and all who sail on her!"

The distraught woman was escorted from the yard and took her own life, along with that of her unborn child, later that day.

Captain Nels Erikson, master of the *Squando*, was not superstitious. Not only did he ignore the screaming woman's threats but he also violated a long tradition of the sea by allowing his wife, Selma, to join him for the maiden voyage.

Although the crew felt that it was bad luck to have a woman aboard, their objections fell on deaf ears.

Captain Erikson had started his career as a whaler and this was his first command of a clipper ship. The route would take them across the Atlantic, around Cape Horn, and into the Pacific to San Francisco. But it became clear that the voyage was doomed soon after the majestic ship cleared the harbor in Oslo.

Selma enjoyed evening strolls on the quarterdeck and soon caught the attention of First Mate Lars Gunderson, who began walking with her each night.

Captain Erikson was a jealous man and became furious upon learning that his wife was socializing with one of his officers. Selma accused Gunderson of stalking her and offering to kill her husband. Erikson confined Selma to her cabin, and it appeared that his explosive behavior had calmed down.

Just before ending the tormented voyage, however, Captain Erikson invited the first mate to his quarters. As Gunderson entered the cabin, a bizarre sight awaited him. Selma was trembling in fear as her jealous husband waved a cutlass and shouted wild accusations. As Erikson swung the cutlass, one sweep of the blade cleanly severed the first mate's head.

After the ship docked in San Francisco, the police fished Gunderson's corpse from the bay. They found his head in a wooden bucket under the captain's bunk.

Nels Erikson was found guilty of murder and was hanged.

The *Squando*'s jinx was still in force as she began the long voyage home in November 1884. The new captain was killed when the crew staged a mutiny.

Frightened crewmen often saw a headless sailor pacing the deck during lonely nights at sea.

The third captain slipped and suffered a broken neck in Oslo Harbor.

The next skipper became a victim of blood poisoning and died in July 1885.

Bad luck followed the ship during the next few

years as the hapless vessel survived a collision with another ship and ran aground twice.

In 1901, the *Squando* began a journey across the Atlantic but never reached her destination. She and her crew vanished, and her fate remains one of the great mysteries of the sea.

The Greenstone Earrings

Leah was beautiful, highly educated and cultured, and part Maori—the race of native people who live in New Zealand. But she was not one to believe in the old Maori ways or follow the ancient traditions.

In time, however, when life became hard for Leah—marriage troubles, small children to raise, and no money—her mother handed down the family treasure, a pair of pear-shaped greenstone earrings, which had been handed down for generations from mother to daughter. The earrings were said to be magical, instant luck changers and protectors, but they were also *tapu*—endowed with strange, inexplicable powers that were not to be taken lightly. They had to be treated with care and in accord with Maori laws. *Never* were they to pass

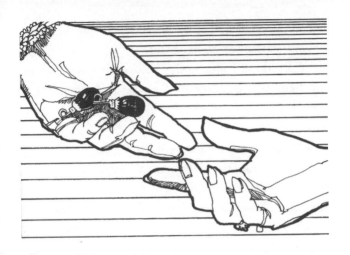

out of the family. If no one was alive to inherit them, they were to be buried with their owner.

When Leah got the earrings, her life changed immediately. Within three months her divorce went through, she remarried, and she was enormously happy.

So when she saw her dear friend Dorothy Crombie, who had moved away from Rotorua to live in Auckland, she impulsively pressed the magnificent earrings into her hand.

"Take these," she said, "with my thanks for all the help you gave me during the bad times. May they bring you the wonderful luck that they have brought me."

That same day an accident happened.

Leah's youngest daughter, a two-year-old, had been playing on the floor when a large pair of scissors somehow detached themselves from the nail they'd been hanging on and sailed across the room, striking the child just above the nose. She still has the scars.

The whole family started to get sick. Leah's oldest son, Wayne, was first—diagnosed with appendicitis. The problem turned out to be a large growth in his abdomen that returned after every operation removed it, baffling the doctors. He was not expected to recover.

When Leah's friend Dorothy heard about these difficulties, she was determined to return the earrings, but she was told that she had to return them the same way she'd gotten them, by placing them in the hands. Leah lived too far away.

Dorothy took up the earrings and spoke to them.

"I promise you that you will go home," she told the earrings, "when I return to Rotorua in just a few months."

As she spoke, the earrings went translucent for a moment, as if there were light held behind them, and then they turned to the side, showing their edges. When Dorothy told Maori friends about this later, they said, yes, that the earrings were telling her they were pleased to go home; they would do this only once.

Soon after that Dorothy received a note from Leah, asking for the earrings back. Evidently, things were getting worse and worse.

Dorothy and her husband got back to Rotorua within two weeks. When they arrived, Leah would not take the earrings back herself. Because she had given them away, she said, they were no longer hers.

Dorothy could only give them to Leah's eldest daughter, Marion, who was six at the time.

Dorothy noticed that one of Marion's eyes was twisted. This disease, Leah had found out, was part of the *tapu*, and it would have traveled through the family until everyone had died, if the earrings had not been returned.

Leah also reported that an hour after she received Dorothy's telegram, she heard from the hospital that her son Wayne had recovered. He was now home with them all.

Wayne proudly showed his scars. They were wide apart—in the shape of a pair of earrings.

Almost everyone has experienced some peculiar feeling or event, or heard a fantastic tale from a thoroughly reliable source. And when it happens to you— or to someone you trust—the occurrence is hard to ignore. Even when it is extremely strange.

The Great Wheel of Light

Phantom ships, sea serpents, mysterious sounds and lights can seem ridiculous to those who did not witness them. But to those who encounter such unusual phenomena, they are very real indeed.

So real are they that they are sometimes recorded in ships' logs, set down in the matter-of-fact language of seafaring men. Such an entry was made on June 10, 1909, in the log of the Danish steamship *Bintang*.

As the *Bintang* steamed through the night in the Strait of Malacca, between Sumatra and the Malay Peninsula, the captain was astonished to see what appeared to be a long beam of light under the water. Like the beam of a searchlight, it seemed to be sweeping across the floor of the sea. The beam

passed across the sea before him and was followed by another and then another, like the revolving spokes of a wheel, or the searchlight beams you sometimes see following one another across the sky.

Soon, some distance from the ship, there appeared a brighter spot or hub that seemed to be the point from which the beams of light originated. The beams revolved silently as the rotating "wheel" slowly approached the *Bintang*. In the words of the captain, "Long arms issued from a center around which the whole system appeared to rotate."

The great revolving wheel was so huge that only half of it could be seen above the horizon. As it revolved toward the *Bintang*, the crew stared in amazement. The long arms of light could not possibly be a reflection of their own light, and there was no other ship in sight.

As the great silent revolving wheel of underwater light came nearer, it seemed to sink lower into the water and grow dimmer. Finally it vanished deep beneath the waves, and the Strait of Malacca was once more black and empty.

A record of this strange encounter has been published by the prestigious Danish Meteorological Institute, but no one knows what it was the bewildered men saw that night.

Duty, Honor, and Valor

In 1885, Geronimo went on a deadly spree of looting and murder throughout the Southwest. Scores of U.S. Cavalry troops vainly tried to halt the Apaches, who left in their wake an appalling number of dead and mutilated settlers. But the Apache warriors moved like the wind and eluded General George Crook's soldiers.

Geronimo's rampaging followers fled into Mexico to escape confrontation with Crook's troopers, who quickly began scouting the border.

In Mexico, Major Carlos Fernandez was sure that the Apaches would attempt to find a way back into Arizona. He and his twelve troops had been chasing a band of Apaches toward the border for eight days. The major was a highly experienced combat

veteran who had been awarded several medals for leadership under fire.

Major Fernandez led his weary soldiers close to an Apache camp where he and a private went on a scouting mission. They ran into a small group of Indians and the private was killed in the ensuing battle. Fernandez made it back to his men, who wondered how their leader had managed to escape. His tattered uniform was bloody and a thin line of crimson liquid trickled down under his dusty cap.

Fernandez had clearly received a dangerous head wound but he refused all attempts to be treated. He waved his men away and pulled the cap down to his eyelashes.

The Apaches attacked that afternoon and the battle continued until sundown. At dawn both sides were again firing, and fighting continued until the Apaches abandoned the battleground. Remarkably, none of the soldiers had died during the exhausting conflict.

Major Fernandez assembled his men and rode into the nearest town. He sat tall in the saddle for a moment, said, "Thank God, my work is done," and then fell to the ground.

The sergeant ran to his commander and checked

for a pulse but found none. As the soldiers gathered around their fallen leader, the sergeant removed the major's cap. They gasped and made the sign of the cross upon their chests when they saw a blood-encrusted bullet hole in the major's forehead—a mortal wound he had received while scouting the Apache camp.

During the past two days, as the valiant soldiers held off a force nearly three times greater than they had anticipated, they had been led by a dead man.

The Christmas Quilt

In 1957, the day before her daughter Florence came to visit, Mrs. Monroe pulled out the old box containing the patchwork quilt. She had found it in the top of a closet when she and her husband bought the Poy Sippi, Wisconsin, farmhouse two years earlier. It was a charming old-fashioned quilt, red and yellow and beautifully handmade, but she had never put it out on a bed before. What was she waiting for?

When Florence arrived, she admired the quilt, and went to bed that night expecting to get a good night's sleep. But that's not what happened.

At about midnight, she woke up with a start as the quilt was jerked away from her. She grabbed onto it with both hands, but the quilt kept pulling away as if someone was at the other end of it, and a woman's

voice said, "Give me back my Christmas quilt."

Florence was petrified. There was no one there, but the tugging didn't stop and neither did the voice. Florence held on to the quilt all night. It

wasn't until dawn that the tugging stopped.

That was the beginning. Soon everyone wanted to test out the quilt.

The first one was Mrs. Monroe's other daughter, Margaret, who brought her own daughter with her. They gave up on the quilt shortly after midnight when it got painfully hot.

Margaret's 18-year-old son was next. He was sleeping on a couch and got his cousin Richard to watch from a roll-away bed they had set up across the room. Right after midnight, Richard saw the quilt pull itself off Tom. He said that it raised up about 12 inches and floated toward the foot of the couch, landing on the floor.

Margaret's daughter had a boyfriend who gave it a try. When, at about midnight, the quilt started to move, he jumped out of bed. Then the cover straightened itself until it was as smooth as if the bed had just been made.

A cousin from California had the quilt sent out there so that her family could try it. The quilt got very hot, she reported in a letter that she sent back with the quilt, whenever anyone tried to sleep under it. They also heard footsteps, as if someone was "running around the house in his bare feet."

Finally, Mr. Monroe put the quilt on his own bed. At first, when he felt the tugging, he hung on to it. Then, he thought, why not let go and see what happens?

"The crazy thing dragged itself across the floor," he said "and curled up under the dresser."

The Christmas quilt, after being sent here and there and "tried" by person after person, finally got the last laugh.

On Halloween, in 1963, the *Oshkosh Northwestern* sponsored a ghost hunting event, in which two women would sleep under the quilt while three other women stood guard.

The Christmas quilt did absolutely *nothing*.

In the end, the ghost or the poltergeist or the entity that so loved the Christmas quilt got its way. None of the family members wanted it on the bed. So the Christmas quilt was put out strictly for show—and given a wide berth.

The Wedding Ring

Ever since her husband, Charley, had been sent overseas to serve as a bomber pilot, Betty Rae "S." of Jackson, Mississippi, had stayed home listening to the radio and staring at Charley's picture. She only went out for groceries or to the church across the street where she prayed for Charley. She never missed a chance to pray for Charley.

One night, she woke to hear church bells ringing. It was after midnight. She got up and looked out the window. The church was all lit up and she could hear the congregation signing.

She was irritated as she hurried into her clothes. Saturday night was a weird time to call a prayer meeting, but she would have gone if she'd known about it. And how come the whole town knew about

this one and Reverend Hawkins never told her?

Betty Rae rushed into the church and sat quickly inn one of the pews. It wasn't Reverend Hawkins up there at the pulpit, but whoever it was, he could certainly offer up a good sermon.

It was odd, she thought, looking around, that she

281

didn't recognize any of the people in the church. Probably it was a visiting evangelist and these people must be his followers.

Someone handed Betty Rae the collection plate. But, in her rush, she hadn't brought any money with her. She took the plate and passed it to the woman on her right.

"No, sister," the usher said loudly. "You didn't put anything in the plate."

"I didn't bring any money," Betty Rae said, "I'm really sorry."

"I'm sorry, too," the usher said unpleasantly, "but you've got to put something in the plate."

People began turning around and gawking at her.

"What's the trouble there, Brother Sam?" asked the preacher from the pulpit.

"This sister doesn't want to put anything in the plate," the usher said.

"Sister," the preacher bellowed, "you've got to put something in the plate!"

The church was buzzing.

"What can I do?" Betty Rae said. "I have nothing with me."

"You have your wedding ring," the usher said. "Put that in the plate."

"No, no!" Betty Rae screamed. "I can't do that!"

"Put the ring in the plate, Sister," thundered the preacher.

"Put the ring in the plate! Put the ring in the plate!" the congregation was chanting.

All eyes were on her. Betty Rae was trembling. She pulled the ring off her finger and dropped it in the collection plate. And suddenly she was filled with despair beyond anything she had ever known.

"Betty Rae, Betty Rae!" It was Reverend Hawkins' voice. He was bending down and looking into her face. "What are you doing here?"

Betty Rae straightened up. "Oh, this is terrible!" she shuddered. "I must have fallen asleep at the prayer meeting!"

"What prayer meeting?" asked Reverend Hawkins. And how in the world did you get in here? I locked up yesterday afternoon and just unlocked the door this morning.

Betty Rae explained to Reverend Hawkins what had happened, and she was in tears again as she talked about the ring.

Reverend Hawkins went up to the front of the church and brought back one of the collection plates. There, sticking to the felt on the bottom of the plate, was her ring.

Monday morning, Betty Rae received the telegram that informed her that Charley had been killed when his plane went down over the English Channel. It must have happened at just about the time Betty Rae put her wedding ring in the collection plate.

The Runaway Locomotive

In January, 1892, engineer J. M. Pinkney visited his friend, a seasoned engineer on the old Northern Pacific Eastbound Overland train. Pinkney's friend covered a stretch of track that crosses the Cascade Mountains of the northwest United States.

As the friends sat together in the engineer's cab of the locomotive, they regaled each other with harrowing accounts that had occurred on their lines. Pinkney enjoyed most of the stories, but he couldn't take them seriously when they featured the paranormal. As hardheaded a man as you could find, he certainly didn't believe in ghosts.

As the train neared Eagle Gorge, the most dangerous spot on the 2,500-mile run, the engineer embarked on the story of old Tom Cypher. Cypher, he said, was an engineer who had died in an accident here two years before.

Suddenly, the engineer grasped the throttle and threw it over, reversing the engine. Then he applied the air brakes, bringing the train to a standstill. The spot where he had stopped was just a few feet short of the place where Cypher had met his death.

Pinkney couldn't understand why the engineer had stopped the train. There had been no hint of any danger. The night was clear and the track was empty. The engineer explained vaguely that some of the machinery had shaken loose and had to be tightened. In a few minutes, he said, they would be on their way.

As they started forward once more, Pinkney pointed out that there had been nothing wrong with the machinery, so why the stop?

"Look there!" his friend told him. "Don't you see it?"

Staring out of the cab window, Pinkney saw the headlights of a locomotive just 300 yards ahead. Shocked, he automatically reached for the lever to stop the train. His friend pushed his hand away, laughing.

"It's only old Tom Cypher's engine, No. 33," he said. "We won't collide. Because that man at the throttle is Cypher himself and, dead though he may be, he can go faster backward than any man alive can go forward. I've seen him 20 times before. Every engineer on this road looks for it.

Pinkney felt the hairs on his neck stand up as he watched the engine ahead of them, its headlights throwing out rays of red, green, and white light. It had begun running silently backward, remaining only a short distance ahead of them. Pinkney glimpsed a shadowy figure at the throttle. Then the locomotive rounded a curve and disappeared from view.

The train on which Pinkney was riding now began passing several small stations. At each one, the station master, fearful of an impending collision, warned the engineer to watch out for a runaway engine, No. 33, that was traveling backward just a short distance ahead of them.

The engineer only laughed. "It's just old Cypher playing a prank," he said.

Pinkney still couldn't believe that a ghost had been at the throttle of that locomotive. Worried, he sent a telegram to the next station, which was in the town of Sprague, asking if No. 33 with a daredevil engineer aboard had been stopped.

The strange reply came back. "Rogue locomotive No. 33 has just arrived, her coal exhausted, her boxed burned out. No engineer at the throttle."

Strange Journeys

How does a man drive through a patch of fog and end up on another continent? What mysterious force is strong enough to lift a man off the ground and transport him to an entirely different location? The following tales contain some of the strangest and most unexplainable journeys ever experienced.

289

The Long Way Home

On the night of June 3, 1968, Dr. Gerardo Vidal and his wife, Raffo, drove to a family reunion in Chascomus, a town along National Route 2, 75 miles south of Buenos Aires in Argentina. After a sumptuous dinner at the home of Martin Rapallini, they left around midnight to begin the journey home to Maipu. They were following another couple, who were their relatives as well as neighbors.

The first couple arrived safely and became worried when the Vidals did not return. Perhaps the Vidals were stranded on the road with a flat tire or car trouble.

Although it was very late, the first couple decided to search for their missing relatives. They carefully retraced the entire route to Rapallini's home in

Chascomus without finding a trace of Gerardo or Raffo. A call to local hospitals revealed that no accident victims had been admitted that night.

One fact had been learned after the long, tiring drive back to Maipu early that morning. The Vidals had vanished without a trace.

Two days later, Martin Rapallini received a phone call from Gerardo Vidal. He was calling from the Argentine embassy in Mexico City, Mexico! Gerardo assured his friend that he and his wife were safe and that they were flying back to Buenos Aires.

When Gerardo and Raffo stepped off the airliner the next day, they were wearing the same clothes they had worn on the Tuesday morning of their disappearance. Raffo was admitted to a private clinic for a severe case of nerves.

Gerardo explained that when he and his wife had driven away from the suburbs of Chascomus on their way back to Maipu, they were listening to music on the radio and maintaining a safe distance from the taillights of their relatives' car.

Suddenly, the Vidals' car drove into a thick fog. Gerardo was confused by the swirling mist and quickly slowed down. That's the last thing he and his wife remembered until regaining consciousness the following morning.

They woke up, still inside the car but on an unfamiliar road. Gerardo opened the door and was astonished to find that all the paint had been scorched from his vehicle.

He stopped several passing motorists to ask for directions to Buenos Aires. All the drivers stared at him as though he were demented, and Gerardo looked back at them as if they were joking about where he was. They must be wrong. He could not possibly be in Mexico.

During the flight to Buenos Aires, Gerardo vainly sought to discover how he and his wife had traveled nearly 4,000 miles overnight to another continent-in their car.

The Reluctant Deserter

On the morning of October 25, 1593, Gil Perez was assigned to guard duty in Manila in the Philippines. Upon arrival at the palace he was arrested when his strange uniform instantly caught the attention of a suspicious officer.

Perez was confused and stared at his surroundings as though he was dreaming.

"Who are you?" asked the officer.

"I am Gil Perez and I was sent to guard the governor's palace in Manila," he said, his eyes reflecting fear. "This place is a palace but not one I know about."

Gil Perez was thrown into jail and questioned relentlessly. He had no answers but wanted to ask a few questions himself. The perplexed sentry

could not comprehend what had happened, and was completely baffled at finding himself in Mexico City.

"What brings you here?" The Mexican officer was sure that Perez was a spy, but he couldn't understand the reason for his presence. "How did you get here?"

"The governor of the Philippines was assassinated last night," explained Perez, "and I was ordered to report to the palace for guard duty." The nervous soldier was unable to explain how he had traveled 9,000 miles overnight from Manila to the Plaza Mayor in Mexico City.

Two months passed before a Spanish brigadier arrived with the tragic report from the Philippines. Mexican authorities then learned the fate of His Excellency, Don Gomez Perez Dasmarinas, the governor of the Philippines. The eminent statesman had been killed by mutinous sailors during a military expedition against the Moluccas.

The official documents also confirmed that the AWOL soldier from the Philippines was telling the truth. The governor had died the night before Gil Perez was found wandering in the plaza, wearing a foreign uniform and a confused expression.

A Walk to the Store

When Sidney Walker left his house on the evening of June 14, 1976, he could not know he would not see his family for a month.

The 33-year-old man, who lived in a city near Rio de Janeiro in Brazil, was on his way to a local cafe for cigarettes and arrived shortly after seven o'clock. After Walker left, the owner realized he had given him the wrong change and hurried outside just in time to see an unidentified glowing object hovering above his customer. The horrified proprietor stood paralyzed as he watched a beam of light engulf Walker, who then vanished.

Sidney Walker's family became worried when he did not return. A few days later, Sidney's brother posted a missing persons notice in the newspaper *O Dia*.

One month to the day of Walker's disappearance,

his distraught family received a letter from the missing man, who said he was in Bairro do Dix-Sept Rosado, Natal—more than 1,200 miles away! He explained that he needed money to get home.

Sidney Walker was soon returned to Rio de Janeiro and placed in a hospital for observation. His confused behavior worried his family as doctors performed various tests.

Walker's bewildered condition finally returned to normal and he explained the reason for his long absence. Upon leaving the cafe on the night he vanished, an unknown force began lifting him. He struggled to free himself but soon became unconscious. He awoke under a grove of coconut palm trees in Natal.

Walker was found by an elderly couple, who invited him to rest in their house. Three weeks later, he recovered his memory and sent a letter to his family.

Sidney Walker had no other recollection of his frightening ordeal.

E veryone has had dreams that are so vivid they would swear they were real. But what about dreams that actually are real? Do dreams allow us to see events that we would otherwise know nothing about? The stories in this chapter are about dreams that came true . . . down to the last detail.

Flight Plan to Oblivion

Few airplanes have been in service on a regular basis for more than four decades, but the Hercules is among those still on active duty with the armed forces.

The transport version, designated C-130, rolled off the production line at Lockheed Aircraft Company in 1952 and went to the Tactical Air Command. This rugged four-engine turboprop has served as a troop carrier, air tanker, search plane, gunship, and in other roles vital to national defense. Various models have been added to the air force inventory over the years. Among them is the WC-130.

An aircrew must have tremendous faith in the airplane it flies into typhoons. The WC-130 is such a warrior, designed to penetrate the most violent weather systems.

One pilot stationed in Europe had a nightmare about a friend who was stationed at Andersen Air Force Base on Guam, a tiny island in the western Pacific. The two men had been college roommates and had flown together after receiving their air-force pilot wings.

The young officer was disturbed by the vision of his friend's WC-130 crashing into the sea with no survivors. Logic told him it had only been a bad dream, but he could not shake the eerie feeling. He called the operations officer in Guam and asked if any planes had gone down.

"We have a C-130 that's overdue," came the reply, "but we don't know very much. At this time, we're listing it as missing."

"It's not a C-130 cargo version," insisted the tense pilot. "It's a weather ship, a WC-130, and it crashed at sea while chasing a typhoon. No one got out." He added the doomed pilot's name as well as the aircraft's serial number just as he had seen it in his frightening dream.

Later that day, the official report confirmed that a WC-130 had been lost while tracking a typhoon over the Pacific. The anxious pilot's friend had been the plane commander, and perished with his crew.

The Iron Tomahawk

This weird incident took place recently in northern Vermont, near the Canadian line, and its authenticity was sworn to by the farmer to whom it happened.

According to his story, when he was a very young boy in 1910, he was greatly intrigued by tales of the Native Americans who had once lived near his home. Every corner of the woods had some historic spot and some accompanying legend about the deeds of daring and terror that had taken place there.

The farmer's boyhood excitement and interest was rekindled one day 30 years later when he found an old iron tomahawk in a gravel pit near where he used to play after school. He carved a crude handle out of wood and attached it to the tomahawk, and this became his most treasured possession. One day he "lost" it. How it came to be lost is a weird story. How it was found again is even more unbelievable.

One night, the farmer dreamed he was a small boy again, coming home from school. Suddenly, a Native American was chasing him, threatening him, following him all the way. When he got home, his parents were out, and he had to face the Native American alone. To save his life he grabbed the old tomahawk and struck the Native American a great blow in the head, killing him instantly and just in time.

In the dream he dragged his attacker out into the pasture and buried him so his parents would not find the body in the house. The dream was so real and so vivid that the next day the farmer rather sheepishly went to the pasture to see if it just could have been true. Of course, there was no sign of any grave or digging, and he felt much relieved. When asked where he had been, he laughingly told his grown children about his dream, and they kidded him about it long afterward.

Strangely enough, he could not find his prized

tomahawk from that night on, no matter where he looked for it.

Just a few years ago, the farmer happened to cross the same corner of the pasture and to his astonishment noticed a shallow depression in the sod exactly where he dreamed he had buried his attacker. He was startled and a bit disturbed, but put it aside as a natural sinking of the land. Still, he could not get it out of his mind.

For weeks he fought off an urge to dig at that spot. Finally, more in jest that in expectation, he got a spade and went to work, hoping no one would see him. He was glad no one had, for a few feet down he came across a skeleton. In the skull was buried an iron tomahawk with a crude wooden handle. *It was the handle he had whittled himself.*

According to the farmer, he filled in the hole and to this day he never revealed the spot to anyone. Who could blame him?

The Fateful Salute

People who dream about dying in a certain manner, and then avoid the situation to prevent the dream from coming true, will never know if the omen had any meaning. But sometimes a clever person who takes every precaution finds that fate always has the last word.

In July 1750, Robert Morris, Sr., the father of Robert Morris, Jr., who managed the nation's financial affairs during the last two years of the American Revolution, dreamed he would die as a result of cannon fire from a naval ship he was scheduled to visit.

Robert Morris, Sr. was so disturbed by the frightening dream that he canceled his inspection of the vessel.

The naval captain thought prophetic dreams

were nonsense and persuaded Morris to reconsider. He personally guaranteed Morris's safety and promised that no cannons would be fired until the distinguished guest was safely ashore.

A few days later, Robert Morris, Sr. inspected the vessel and stepped into a small boat that would return him to land. The captain again reminded his men that a salute would only occur upon his command.

Robert Morris, Sr. was halfway to shore when a fly began maneuvers around the captain's nose. The captain raised his hand to swat the annoying insect and the cannon crew assumed it was a signal to open fire.

One shot rang out and a tiny piece of shrapnel struck Robert Morris, Sr., wounding him fatally.

Peril on the Sea

In the spring of 1915, Professor I. B. S. Holbourne, the eminent British lecturer, completed a successful tour in the United States and boarded the *Lusitania* at Pier 54 in New York.

The luxurious Cunard liner was ready for sea and equipped with many refinements not yet available in modern hotels, including air-conditioning and cabin phones.

At 12:30 on the afternoon of May 1, a low hum became a muffled roar as the steam turbines turned 4 huge propellers, and the 790-foot liner edged away from the dock.

Captain William Turner was pleased when the morning drizzle was replaced by bright sunlight, sparkling off the liner's white superstructure as they sailed leisurely up the Hudson River.

On May 7, the *Lusitania* sailed into a predawn fog bank about 75 miles off the southwestern tip of Ireland. By eight o'clock the thickening mist caused Captain Turner to reduce speed and signal other ships with the throaty horn.

Shortly after eleven o'clock, the dense fog evaporated and the magnificent ocean liner was bathed by warm sunshine.

Across the Atlantic, during the early hours of the same day, Holbourne's wife, Marion, was reading in their home and fell asleep in the chair. Soon she was dreaming, but the scene was not peaceful. She suddenly found herself on the deck of an elegant liner that was slanting dangerously. Black smoke was streaming from a pair of ventilators near the bridge, and she felt the vessel shudder from a boiler explosion.

Marion watched in fascination as the crew lowered lifeboats and shouted orders. She noticed the passengers' anxiety, but there was no panic as they waited for seats in the boats. Then she heard an ominous creaking as the liner's plates and beams began shifting. The wounded vessel's slant was now nearly 20 degrees, and frantic passengers struggled to keep their balance. Chairs and tables not bolted to the deck began sliding into the sea.

Marion realized the ship was in mortal danger and hailed a young officer. She identified herself and asked if her husband was aboard. The officer shook his head and said that Professor Holbourne had gone belowdecks to offer people life jackets and assistance. He then escorted them topside and helped them into boats before the crew finally ordered him into a lifeboat.

Marion awoke and discussed the dream with her family. They laughed and considered the experience a silly fantasy.

A few hours later, their opinion changed when they heard that the *Lusitania* had become the victim of a German submarine. The U-20, commanded by *Kapitanleutnant* Walter Schwieger, had fired a torpedo into the ocean liner's starboard bow at 2:10 that afternoon. The 32,000-ton vessel sank 18 minutes later. Of the 1,959 people aboard, 760 survived.

News of the shocking incident swept the nation, whose angry citizens had not been so incensed since the news from Paul Revere. The tragic event on the Irish Sea forced the United States into war and changed the course of history.

Marion Holbourne later learned that her husband had assisted many passengers before leaving the stricken ship on orders from the crew—exactly as the young officer had described in her dream.

A Mother's Love

Operation Dynamo at Dunkirk was the greatest evacuation in military history, and its success was possible because the British Army Intelligence was able to intercept and decode messages from the German High Command. Between May 27 and June 4, 1940, an allied naval armada rescued 338,226 troops facing imminent capture by German forces that had surrounded the French city.

Some soldiers did not survive the rescue mission. They died en route to England when their ships were attacked by Luftwaffe planes.

Corporal Teddy Watson was among those listed as missing and his mother, Helen, was sure he had been killed. Many official documents had been lost during the evacuation, and the army had no record of the British soldier's death or burial.

Sixteen years later, Helen realized she would not live much longer, and desperately wanted to find her son's grave.

One night she had a remarkable dream.

She found herself wandering through a military cemetery covered with small white crosses. For no apparent reason, she paused at a particular cross. It was plain and revealed no name or other information. As she stared at the simple marker, her son suddenly appeared. Helen was surprised but not frightened as Teddy smiled and then disappeared.

When Helen awoke, she was certain she could locate her son's final resting place. She traveled from her home in Ellerbeck, England, to Dunkirk and found the cross she had seen in her dream. She pointed it out to the officer who had accompanied her to the cemetery.

Upon returning to England, a letter was waiting in her mailbox. She was pleased to learn that the grave had been opened and examined by military authorities.

It was not necessary to identify the remains from dental records. The rosary, the silver cigarette holder, and the photo in the locket belonged to her son.

Dream of Disaster

Henry Armitt Brown was a lawyer and a lecturer—not the kind of person you'd expect to have a strange psychic encounter. But the dream he had—and the experiences that followed—are not at all what anyone would expect.

It happened in November, 1865, when he was a law student in New York. It was a cold, blustery evening. Henry was in bed before midnight and asleep shortly after. He had hardly lost consciousness when he seemed to hear loud and confused noises and felt a choking sensation at his throat, as if it were being grasped by a strong hand.

He woke up (in the dream) and found himself lying on his back on the cobblestones of a narrow street, struggling beneath the body of a heavy man with long, uncombed hair and a grizzly beard. The man had one hand at Henry's throat and the other was holding his wrists.

Henry realized he was about to be killed, and he fought back furiously. They rolled over on the stones and then he saw the man pick up a shiny—evidently brand new—hatchet. Henry made one last intense effort to get free of his attacker, and, as he did, he saw over the man's shoulder that some of his friends were rushing to his rescue. His closest friend was ahead of the rest and he leaped onto the back of the thug. The hatchet flashed, and Henry felt a dull blow on his forehead. He fell back onto the ground as a numbness spread from his head to his body. A warm liquid flowed down on his face and into his mouth, and he realized it was blood.

Then he seemed to be suspended in the air a few feet over his body, looking at his body on the ground, the hatchet stuck in his head. He could hear the cries of his friends, loud at first and then growing fainter and fading away into silence.

A delightful sensation came over him of relaxation and peace. He heard superb music, smelled wonderful scents and seemed to be lying on a bed of downy softness—when he woke up. He had not been asleep for more than half an hour.

Early the next morning, Henry and his best friend were walking to law school together.

"I had a weird dream about you last night," his friend told him. "I fell asleep about midnight and dreamed that I was passing through a narrow street when I heard noises and cries of murder. Then I saw you lying on your back, fighting off a roughneck who was holding you down. I ran forward, but as I got there, he hit you on the head with a hatchet and killed you instantly. Quite a vivid dream. When I woke up there were tears on my face, believe it or not.

"What was the killer like?" Henry asked.

His friend described the man precisely.

A week later, Henry was visiting another of his friends in New Jersey.

My husband, "the man's wife said," had a horrible

dream about you the other night. He dreamed that you were killed in a street fight. He ran to help you, but before he could reach you, your enemy had hit you with a big club."

"Oh, no," said her husband, coming into the room, "he killed you with a hatchet—a brand new, shiny one, too."

Henry had told no one about his dream, and Henry's two friends did not know each other.

Tales of Terror

Everyone likes a truly chilling ghost story, but these tales are scarier than most. Better not read them when you're alone in the house.

The Deadly
Spirit of Raku-nene

The hot afternoon sun was blazing down on the tropical Gilbert Islands that straddle the equator in the Pacific Ocean. It was 1917, and the war in Europe was grinding hopelessly on, but here all was peaceful.

In his thatched office in the central island of Abemama sat the district officer of the British colonial service, Arthur Grimble. Grimble, a thin, studious man, lifted his head in bewilderment as a high-pitched, wavering cry came floating over the palms. It went on and on—the cry of somebody with seemingly endless breath.

The district officer left his hut and walked slowly through clumps of trees toward the sound. Eventually, he reached the leaf hut of a native con-

stable. Sitting outside the dwelling was a young woman. She was wailing mournfully, but not in anger or pain. Her eyes were staring into space.

He didn't know it then, but Arthur Grimble was looking at a girl who was under a spell of death.

She was only about 17, and obviously in the grip of some mysterious and serious disease. She had become ill, her policeman father told Grimble, at about dawn that day.

When Grimble asked why he wasn't doing anything to help the girl, he was astounded to hear the native reply: "It would be of no use. She is dying. She is being killed by the evil spirit Raku-nene."

Why, the British officer demanded, should the girl have been put under a spell of death? The answer was simple—she had scorned a man who loved her, and he had asked Raku-nene to wreak revenge for him.

Grimble angrily brushed the girl's family aside and dragged her into the hut. There he gave her a sedative. The girl's brother looked on sadly and said: "You waste your time. You cannot fight a spirit with your white powers."

Grimble made the girl as comfortable as he could, but she continued moaning loudly. He demanded to see the lover who had ordered the spirit Raku-nene to put the girl under a death spell.

When he met him, he was surprised to hear the young man admit: "Yes, she scorned me and must pay the penalty. I took a strand of her hair and tied it around my thigh for three days. Then I burned it and called on Raku-nene. This is how it is done."

That night, as the girl lay moaning, her father and brother and other family friends approached her to try to calm her. She seized a knife and attacked them with it, shrieking that she wanted to be left alone. They left her alone and she died the next day. Just before dying she screamed the word "Raku-nene," over and over.

Arthur Grimble went to the family hut and examined her body. He found no trace of disease and no injuries. His official report was that she died of natural causes.

Grimble dismissed the unhappy affair from his mind, but two years later he had cause to remember it: Another woman died in similar circumstances. After her death Grimble spoke to a man he knew had been friendly with her.

The man told him: "She rejected me—she found another. So I called on Raku-nene, as is our custom."

Auto-suggestion? Hypnosis? Grimble found no evidence of either. In fact, the man in this incident told Grimble that he had not informed the woman that he had called on the spirit Raku-nene to place a spell on her.

Again, Grimble found on examination that death appeared due to natural causes.

Later, the British administration learned of so many deaths among Gilbert Island women with no sound reason for them that they ordered penal servitude for anybody found guilty of Raku-nene magic.

Grimble was unwilling to accept the fact that an evil spirit could case the death of a human being. But he did admit: "There is among the island women a sudden form of madness accompanied by physical disfigurement which, in the mind of the victim, is invariably associated with the name Raku-nene."

The Strange Disappearance of Charles Ashmore

Charles Ashmore was 16 years old on the November evening that he stopped outside his home to get some water from the well. He never came back.

It happened in Quincy, Illinois, in 1878. His father and sister went out looking for him with a lantern. They followed his footprints easily in the thin layer of snow that had just fallen. About halfway to the well, the footprints stopped. There was no sign of a struggle or a fall or even a jump or slide. They just stopped.

Really frightened now, the two hurried to the well. It was covered with ice—ice that had been frozen solid for hours. There was no chance that he had fallen in.

His father and sister, mystified, returned home

where the family waited, desperate to have some answer to the puzzle. None came.

For days, Charles' mother walked back and forth along his route from the house to the well, hoping to find some clue to his disappearance.

On the fourth day, she heard her son's voice calling to her. She had been out by the well, but the voice wasn't coming from there. It would come from different directions—sometimes from above, sometimes from the sides. It sounded clear enough, but Charles wasn't there.

"Charlie, where are you? Tell us how to get to you," Mrs. Ashmore kept saying.

But she never got an answer to her questions.

For months afterwards at various times, Charles' voice was heard by other members of the family and by neighbors. It seemed to be coming from a greater distance away, but no one could identify the direction.

Gradually, the voice grew fainter, and by the middle of the summer, no one could hear it at all.

What happened to Charles Ashmore? Did he step into another dimension of time or space? Was he there all the time—beyond reach—unable to find his way home? If not, where did he go?

The Whistle

On a small, isolated farm in South Carolina a woman lived alone with her dog. One night, as she was going about her chores, she became aware of an odd whistling sound somewhere outside. It did not sound like high wind in the pines, noises of nature, or a human whistle. It was very strange. Curious, she went to the door. As she did, she noticed that her small terrier was barking and howling on the back porch. This porch, which was enclosed, made a dark and snug haven for the pup.

She opened the door. The wavering and high-pitched whistle seemed to be coming toward the house from across the hills, yet it was as hard to locate as the chirp of a cricket. It must be some of the local youngsters trying to frighten me, she thought,

but she shut and bolted the door and hastily got her late husband's revolver—just in case. She returned to the door to await whatever might happen next. She left the dog on the back porch. If it was just pranksters, his barking would frighten them away.

The whistle came nearer, although the woman could see nothing. Then it seemed to turn, pass slowly around the house, and approach the porch, where the now-hysterical terrier was beside himself with excitement.

Soon there was a terrific outcry and sounds of struggle on the back porch. Then silence—as complete as it was terrifying. The woman, alone in the stillness, shook with fright. She did not dare go out onto the porch.

Eventually she went to bed.

The next morning she investigated. The dog was gone, and blood was spattered all about. What had taken place? The whistle had stopped when the struggle began. But what was it that had caused the bloodshed? What had happened to the little terrier? Nobody ever found out.

Ghostly Animals

M any people believe that animals can sense the presence of ghosts or other supernatural beings when mere humans are not aware of them. Perhaps it is true. There are many tales about animals who show great fear or love toward someone or something no one else can see. But stories of animal ghosts or animals who are bewitched are a bit less common. Here are a few stories of both kinds.

The Black Dog of Hanging Hills

Many legends have been told of frightening black dogs that haunt deserted roads, gloomy castles, even townhouses. But the black dog of Hanging Hills is gentle and friendly, a splendid companion with whom to spend an afternoon, and he is deadlier than all the rest. If you ever meet him, you'll know him by two peculiar features: One, he leaves no footprints. Two, he seems to bark occasionally, but never makes a sound.

When you see him the first time, he brings you joy. He follows you wherever you go, wags his tail, waits for you if you stop along the way.

The second time you meet him is a time of sorrow for you.

But, if you see him twice, don't go back to

Hanging Hills. Because the third time you see the black dog, you die.

W. H. C. Pynchon told part of the story almost a century ago. A geologist, he was visiting Meriden, Connecticut, because he wanted to see some unusual rock formations he had heard about. When he first saw the black dog, it was standing on a high boulder and looking down at him, wagging its tail. When Pynchon continued on his way, the dog ran alongside. When the geologist stopped at an inn for lunch, the dog waited outside for him. They spent the afternoon together, and it wasn't until dusk that the dog took off into the woods.

Pynchon didn't go back to Hanging Hills for a number of years. When he did it was in February. He went with another geologist, who knew the area fairly well. In fact, his friend had told Pynchon that he had seen the peculiar little dog twice before on his visits.

The next day, the two men began climbing the mountain called West Peak. They chose to squeeze through a gap between two cliffs. It was a particularly dark space that turned out to be rather icy. As they neared the top of the mountain, they looked up and saw the black dog high on the rocks, wagging its tail and barking—without making a sound.

Delighted to see him, they continued their ascent, looking forward to greeting the dog when they got to the top.

Then, unbelievably, Pynchon's friend lost his footing on the ice, and before Pynchon could come to his rescue, smashed down the cliff, crashing violently against the rocks below. It was the third time Pynchon's friend had seen the dog. And the second time for Pynchon, who experienced great sorrow at the loss of his friend.

Later, Pynchon was told the story of the black dog by local people and he wrote about his experience after that. In view of this knowledge, it is difficult to understand why he went back to West Peak to retrace the steps he had already taken with his friend.

But perhaps you've already figured out what happened.

Pynchon's broken body was found in approximately the same spot that his friend's body had been found a couple of years before.

Did he see the black dog? We'll never know for sure. But others have since reported seeing the dog. Pynchon was not the last climber to die on West Peak. The most recent victim died there in 1972 on Thanksgiving Day. How many times do you think the climber had been there before?

The Psychic Horse

The two men could barely keep a straight face as the stable door opened and out shuffled the oldest, boniest horse they had ever seen. This clinched it! Now there was no mistake: The whole thing was a hoax.

On the face of it, the feelings of the men who stood in the stable yard in St. John's, Newfoundland, Canada, in 1955, would have been echoed by anyone with normal, healthy skepticism. For they had been persuaded, despite their better judgment, to seek advice from this pathetic creature on the fate of a missing child.

But within minutes, what appeared to be a joke in rather bad taste was transformed into an uncanny glimpse into the supernatural that no one has ever been able to explain.

It soon became obvious that only one being in the whole of Canada knew what had happened to three-year-old Ronnie Weitcamp. And that was Lady Wonder, a 30-year-old mare, spending the twilight of her days in a stable a hundred miles away.

On October 11, 1955, Ronnie left his three

playmates in the front yard of his home near a Newfoundland naval base and ran around to the back of the house. He disappeared into some nearby woods and, despite the pleas of his playmates, did not come out. As they ran to tell his mother, the child roamed deeper into the woods.

Neighbors scoured the woodland. By midafternoon, the police had been called and a full-scale search mounted. As darkness fell, some 1,500 searchers combed bushes and ravines. The bitter cold descended. They knew that if the child was not found, there was little chance of his surviving the night.

But he wasn't found, and the police, convinced that their search had been thorough, turned to other theories.

Had he been kidnapped? Eleven days passed, and there was no sign of the child.

The tips and leads supplied by the public led nowhere, and hope was almost abandoned. Then a police official remembered that a child had been found years before through information supplied by a horse!

In any other circumstance it would have been laughable, but the police looking for little Ronnie Weitcamp had become desperate, so two detectives were sent to interview the horse.

By any standards, Lady Wonder was a remarkable horse. By the time she was two years old she had learned to count and spell out words by moving children's blocks around.

One day she spelled out *engine* as a huge tractor rumbled past the house. Later, in response to questions, the horse would use her nose to flip large tin letters that hung from a bar across her stall. In this way, she spelled out the answers to questions put to her.

The fame of the horse had spread. Thousands came to seek answers to their queries. She was claimed to have predicted that Franklin D. Roosevelt would be the next president of the United States, before he had even been nominated.

She picked the winners of countless races and,

venturing into the field of mathematics, briskly calculated the cube roots of numbers. University specialists in extrasensory perception spent weeks testing the horse and came away convinced that she had some kind of telepathic powers.

But she remained basically a harmless curiosity until one day, after a four-month search for a seven-year-old-girl, the police turned in desperation to Lady Wonder. She directed them to a water-filled quarry that already had been searched without success. A further hunt led to the child's body, exactly where the horse had indicated.

Coincidence or not, having exhausted their options, the authorities decided it was worth pursuing. But now the horse was old and such tests upset her. After convincing the owner that this was an emergency, the officers were eventually allowed to question Lady Wonder.

The bar of letters was put in place and the questions began. They asked, "Do you know why we are here?" Immediately the horse spelled out *boy*.

Q: Do you know the boy's name?

A: Ronnie.

Q: Is he dead or alive?

A: Dead.

Q: Was he kidnapped?

A: No.

Q: Will he be found?

A: Yes.

Q: Where?

A: Hole.

Q: What is near him?

A: Elm.

Q: What kind of soil?

A: Sand.

Q: When will he be found?

A: December.

That was the end of the interview. Refusing to answer any further questions, the mare tottered away. The detectives telephoned headquarters with the answers and a new search was planned.

A storm of ridicule descended as it became

known the police were acting on the advice of a horse. Naval base officials, particularly, insisted that the grounds had been thoroughly searched and that it was quite obvious that the child had been abducted. A new search was conducted anyway, but nothing was found and the police department began to curse the day they sought the help of Lady Wonder.

Then on the afternoon of Sunday, December 4, the body of Ronnie Weitcamp was found by two boys in a thicket at the bottom of a ravine about a mile from his home. He had not been kidnapped: Medical evidence showed he had died of exposure. He lay in sandy soil, just out of the shade of the nearest tree—a large elm.

Every detail of the horse's prediction had been proved uncannily accurate; it was unbelievable but true. It was also the last time Lady Wonder used the swinging letters.

The following spring, she died, taking with her the mystery of her glimpse into a world few humans have ever penetrated.

Night Ride

This story was told by an old doctor who lived a hermit's life in a small New England village. It happened when he was a young boy, but he told it and retold it in exactly the same way until his death.

When the doctor was 15 years old, his father had a bay colt that he let his son ride. One evening the boy started riding to a nearby town. On the way he had to pass a cottage where a woman by the name of Dolly Spokesfield lived. She was rumored to have unusual powers, skill in the occult arts, and the ability to turn herself into almost anything she wished. She was, it was whispered, a genuine witch of the inner circle—certainly a person to be avoided by anyone out at night alone.

As the lad approached the cottage that belonged to Dolly Spokesfield, he kept to the middle of the

road and urged the colt to a faster trot. But his pre-
cautions were in vain.

As the colt and rider came abreast of the cottage,
a coal-black cat suddenly leaped out of the darkness and landed on the colt's neck. The frightened
horse stopped short, almost throwing the boy over
his head.

The boy tried desperately to get rid of the cat and urged his mount on, beating him with his whip, but the cat held on and the colt refused to move with the vicious cat hissing upon his neck.

The boy was afraid to leave his horse and run. In panic, he dismounted and began to beat the cat with the whip, holding the colt by the bridle rein as it reared and plunged, trying to shake off the terrifying creature.

At last the boy dislodged the cat and hurriedly rode home. The poor colt was bruised and clawed, and apparently exhausted by his ordeal. So injured and frightened was he that the boy was afraid the animal would die before morning. He turned him loose in the barn instead of putting him in the stall and went to bed trembling and fearful that the colt wouldn't last the night.

At dawn, the boy hurried to the barn to inspect the battered and clawed animal. To his amazement, the young horse was in perfect condition. He showed no sign of exhaustion, and nowhere on his body could the boy find a trace of bruises from the whip, a claw mark, or a single reminder of the frantic events of the previous night.

The story has an even stranger ending. A neighbor soon stopped by to report that Dolly Spokesfield had just been found almost dead, her body bruised and beaten as though by a whip. And under two of her fingernails were some short bay hairs, such as you'd find, perhaps, on the neck of a young colt ridden by a frightened boy alone in the night.

Index